Country Towns
of
NEW YORK

Country Towns
of
NEW YORK

Bill Kauffman

illustrated by
Victoria Sheridan

Country Roads Press
CASTINE, MAINE

917.47
KAU
1994

Country Towns of New York
© 1994 by Bill Kauffman. All rights reserved.

Published by Country Roads Press
P.O. Box 286, Lower Main Street
Castine, Maine 04421

Text and cover design by Janet Patterson
Illustrations by Victoria Sheridan
Typesetting by Typeworks

ISBN 1-56626-061-2

Library of Congress Cataloging-in-Publication Data

Kauffman, Bill, 1959–
    Country towns of New York / Bill Kauffman.
        p.   cm.
    Includes bibliographical references and index.
    ISBN 1-56626-061-2 : $9.95
    1. New York (State)—Guidebooks. 2. Cities and towns—New York
(State)—Guidebooks. I. Title.
F117.3.K38 1994
917.4704'43—dc20   93-42263
                                                              CIP

Printed in the United States of America.
10 9 8 7 6 5 4 3 2 1

For Lucine,
my editor and photographer,
who was with me every step of the way,
as she will be on our journey without end.

Contents

Introduction

There is a New York in which only stars scrape the sky. With the exception of Cooperstown, the Valhalla of the American game, its towns do not teem with tourists, its streets are not clogged with cars.

When I moved to Santa Barbara, California, in 1985 the first bumper sticker I saw read, "Welcome to California; Now Go Home." Rural New York, though far more insular and provincial a place than Santa Barbara, is warm and welcoming of visitors. We're an undiscovered country, touristically speaking, with a lode of lore and legend and beauty.

We are, in every sense but geographically, closer to Nebraska than to New York City, but our regional character is markedly different from those of the Middle West or the Mid-Atlantic or even the adjoining New England states.

Historians call the area west of Utica "the Burned-Over District," for in the first half of the nineteenth century this land was ablaze with fiery enthusiasts: reformers and utopians, suffragettes and abolitionists, crackpot preachers and numinous visionaries set our house on fire and the scattered embers and ashes can be seen today. To the east and south was Dutch country, rather more stolid and substantial, less eccentric, stoutly proud. (They ran the Connecticut fool Ichabod Crane out of town in style.)

Yet ours is also a state of contradictions. For every ragtag dreamer and communer with the dead there were a dozen industrious farmers; New York sent the most men per capita to the Union army but it was also the hotbed of antiwar, anti-Lincoln activity.

Small-town New York today, though less volatile, is still a strikingly variegated place. A Mormon theatrical extravaganza takes place amidst roadside apple stands; the manorial home of a wartime president is across the street from a drive-in theater; a feminist park is nestled in a working-class Finger Lakes town.

"York State is a country," insisted Carl Carmer, one of our finest regional writers. We've given the world Millard Fillmore and Franklin D. Roosevelt, Elbert Hubbard and Frederic Remington, Jell-O and Welch's Grape Juice. Our country is many things, but it is not forgettable. See for yourself.

Thanks to the many fine people who took the time to chat or correspond or otherwise share their knowledge with me. For their many kindnesses I am especially grateful to Bill and Martha Treichler, publishers of the *Crooked Lake Review* in Hammondsport. The Treichlers met at Black Mountain College in North Carolina; with their generosity, their hard work, their independence, their curiosity, and their delightful hospitality they embody the best tradition of family-based American bohemianism. I also thank Lucine Kauffman, John Rezelman, Ed Harris, Bob and Mary Lou Koch, Warren Hunting Smith, Henry W. Clune, Peter H. Clune, Suzanne and Bob Jones, Mary Baker, Mike and Cathy Kauffman, Joe and Sandy Kauffman, Victoria Kauffman, Wendell Tripp, Barb and Ken Shephard, Bill Kelty, Gary D. Grote, Thomas J. Prittie, Ann Marie Brust, Dick Compo, Chuck and Margie Ruffino, Mary S. Dibble, Marie Andonian, and everyone else who assisted me as I drove the roads—paved and otherwise—of my New York, so rich in heritage, so blessed with natural beauty, and so overflowing with goodwill and neighborliness.

1

Palmyra

Leave the New York State Thruway at Exit 43 and drive seven miles north on State 21, or take State 31 east from Rochester for twenty miles.

The sacred and the profane meet in Palmyra, a gnarled old Erie Canal town in which a visionary named Joseph Smith claimed to have received, from an angel named Moroni, a set of gold tablets inscribed with the Book of Mormon.

Drumlins—hills and ridges formed by glacial drift, unearthly cones left by the ice that covered the region in its primordium—surround the village; the Hill Cumorah, site of Smith's revelation, is a drumlin. But Palmyra has two histories. One is earthy, filled with the blood, sweat, and tears that built the canal; the other is religious and Utopian. The stark contrast makes for a fascinating duality in this village.

The 363-mile-long Erie Canal, built between 1817 and 1825, is a marvel of engineering and bullwork. It was the first great public works project in America. Opponents called it "Clinton's ditch," after Governor DeWitt Clinton, and in truth its effects were not all salutary. It disrupted the rhythms of agrarian York and acted as a subsidy to favored businesses. No matter: the canal, with its rough-hewn characters, its Paddies and Mollys and mules named

1

Sal, was the central mythographic event in our history. And no town drew more of its vim and vitality from the Great Ditch than Palmyra—or "Pal" to canallers.

(First, an explanation. Our forbears in upstate New York called the state "York" and themselves "Yorkers." The prefix *New* was for the city slickers down in Babylon on the Hudson.)

Palmyra was the setting of *Canal Town* (1944), a novel by the prolific Samuel Hopkins Adams, the legendary muckraking journalist of the 1920s who spent his autumnal years on the shores of Lake Owasco, thirty-five miles to the east.

Canal Town, set in the Palmyra of the 1820s, is not one of Mr. Adams' better books. It's much inferior to *Rome Haul* and *Erie Water*, the classic canal novels of Boonville's Walter D. Edmonds. Yet Adams' tale may interest those who want to walk the towpath or skim stones along the stagnant waters of DeWitt Clinton's ditch. He concludes: "There came a day when, incredibly, the Grand Canal, that utmost achievement of Man the Engineer, diminished to a negligible agency of the nation's traffic, as the swift trains sped, hooting disdainfully, across an expanding land. Today Palmyra fulfills its quiet destiny, toiling and sleeping beside its inland waters, one of a thousand small communities, pioneers and monuments of a past in which they played an ardent part in the growth of a new America."

Well, Palmyra may have quieted some since the days of brawling canallers and visionary prophets, but the old town still has life—and charm.

As you enter Palmyra on State 31 from the west, you'll see the Erie Canal Aqueduct. Built in 1856, as the canal was being renovated, its stone block arches have a kind of majesty to them. This is what engineers mean when they speak of art. The aqueduct carries the canal waters over the Ganargua Creek, and you can grab a ringside seat in the Wayne County Park. There are picnic facilities and bike trails and patient kids angling for sunfish along the banks. Pack a lunch—okay, I'll drop the pastoral pose—pick up a burger and fries and get alimentary beside the canal. (An atrocious pun, I know.)

The highlight of Palmyra's year, at least for those domiciled elsewhere, is Canaltown Days, which spans a weekend in September. Main Street is given over to an enormous craft show and flea market, and the aroma of grilled hots and Italian sausages and hamburgers adds a nice pungency to the late summer air. An antique show fills the elementary school on Canandaguia Street, and the Garden Club usually sponsors a tour of noteworthy homes.

Canallers, as a rule, were not devout, but Palmyrans were; the evidence exists at the corner of Main and State 21, where the Baptist (built in 1870), Methodist (1867), Presbyterian (1832), and Episcopalian (1861) churches stand on each of the four corners. *Ripley's Believe It or Not* even reported this holy quadrangle in its pages.

The Western Presbyterian is particularly attractive: a Federal-style church fronted by four massive pillars, it was designed by

The Erie Canal Aqueduct over Ganargua Creek

Abner Lakey and restored in 1949. You're more than welcome on any Sunday morning of the year, rain or shine.

The Village Park is eastward on the same block. Check out the bandstand, one of the last in the state, built by Pliny T. Sexton, a banker and leading citizen of the town. One old-timer told me of Pliny: "At one time he owned half of Palmyra—he foreclosed on everybody!" (He even owned the Hill Cumorah.) In keeping with our holy theme, we'll remember Pliny not for his avarice but by his green, serene park. Sexton's home, which still stands at the corner of Main and Fayette streets, was once a stop on the Underground Railroad.

Flanking the bandstand is a Spanish cannon taken from the ship *Oquendo*, which was destroyed in the Battle of Santiago during the Spanish-American War. Rear Admiral William T. Sampson, an Annapolis man from Palmyra, commanded the North Atlantic Fleet in that not-so-splendid little war. The admiral, a leading naval strategist and tireless crusader for a steel navy, is buried in Arlington National Cemetery; his boyhood home is the gracious white colonial with the big porch at 112 Vienna Street. (Just take a right on Mill Street, off Main, and look for the house at the foot of Mount Prospect.)

A cluster of museums graces downtown Palmyra. First up, at 122 Williams Street, just off Main, is the Alling Coverlet Museum, home of the largest collection (250-plus) of handwoven coverlets in the United States.

Coverlets are often referred to as the "American Tapestry." Though spun for the most prosaic of functions—to cover the bed—many of the these wool, cotton, or linen creations are florid, ornate, and vivid. They average ninety inches in length and eighty inches in width and were made by housewives and professional weavers alike (Palmyran Ira Hasdell was a nineteenth-century master of this art). The American coverlet heyday was during the first seventy-five years of the republic, before the Civil War and the nation's consequent industrialization.

Mrs. Harold Alling, a Rochesterian, donated more than 200 coverlets to the museum that bears her name. Fifty or so are displayed at any one time in this two-story former print shop; be sure to see the red and white "E Pluribus Unum" woven in 1849 by Palmyran James Van Ness. The museum sets aside one room for that coverlet cousin, the quilt, and another for the iridescent miniature rugs made between 1912 and 1922 by Sarah Hall Bonesteele of nearby Victor. A gift and bookshop is in the lobby.

Walk back up Williams to Main Street, turn left, and step into the Grandin Building, once home to the printing business that published the first copies of the Book of Mormon in 1830. The Mormon Church has refurbished the building, which includes oil portraits of namesake Egbert Bratt Grandin and his wife Harriet Rogers Grandin painted by the western New York artist Alonzo Parks. Exhibits depicting the development of the Latter-day Saints line the walls; a kindly church elder is on hand and, believe you me, he will not be loath to answer any questions about Mormonism. The Grandin Building is open every day and is packed at Hill Cumorah time.

Take the first left past the Grandin Building down to 132 Market Street. The Palmyra Historical Museum, which still bears traces of its former incarnation as the St. James Hotel, contains a large collection of nineteenth-century furniture and Palmyra artifacts. Tours are more or less self-guided; ask the attendant to blow the canal whistle, which sends neighborhood dogs scurrying for cover. The museum has some fine Erie Canal art and lots of portraits of Palmyrans looking somber—yes, Pliny Sexton is represented, eyes glinting in anticipation of foreclosing on some indolent mechanic. What struck us is how little the old Palmyra, as seen in a variety of photos, differs from the new Palmyra. The continuity is reassuring.

Almost next door, at 140 Market Street, is one of the oddest and most delightful out-of-the-way museums you'll ever find, the William Phelps General Store. The Phelps family ran a successful emporium from the late 1860s until the 1940s in this circa-1845 brick structure with a cast-iron balcony.

The store was killed with the advent of the supermarket. It is preserved as the Phelps family left it, shelves full of raspberry extract and elixirs; this is okay as it goes, but then you go upstairs, to the sprawling living quarters, where until 1976 the village eccentric, Miss Sybil Phelps, lived without electricity or plumbing and with a menagerie of curs and shrieking cats. Water damage discolors the walls; Queen Anne Eastlake furniture shares rooms with threadbare clothing and upholstery ripped to shreds by incorrigible kittens. The hole in the attic floor through which Sybil, a dedicated spiritualist, communed with her dead father, beckons, drawing our attention away from the exquisite woodworking.

Two charming elementary schoolgirls led us through the Phelps Museum, and they spoke so familiarly of Sybil—"she was sooo ugly"; "she let those animals run wild"; "she had an artist carve occult signs into her bedpost to speak to her relatives"—that we wished we knew the old bird. Anyone who has ever feared a wizened grimalkin in a spooky house down the street must visit the Phelps Museum.

All the museums (except the Grandin Building) are run by Historic Palmyra and are open from June until October. Admission is free, though you'll probably want to make a donation.

Like most small upstate towns, Palmyra is made for walking. Take a leisurely stroll down Cuyler Street, one block parallel to State 21. Among its distinguished edifices is the Palmyra King's Daughter's Free Library, once home to the Carlton H. Rogers family. Palmyra legend has it that Mark Twain, a guest of the Rogers', attended a stag dinner in Pliny T. Sexton's honor and heard at that soiree of a local rascal named Finn McCool who picked huckleberries. The rest was history. Well, at least myth-history. Shortly after our trip to Palmyra I was at a picnic with Professor Herbert Wisbey of Elmira, a Twain scholar. He scoffed at the tale, and gave me the January 1988 edition of the Mark Twain Society Bulletin, which he edits. A historian named Betty Trososky thoroughly debunked the Finn McCool story; indeed, Twain probably never even visited Palmyra. Besides, jibed Mrs. Trososky, good old Pliny, who seldom "gave even a smile a year," was unlikely to inhabit the same planet, let alone the same room, as Mr. Twain (or his alter ego, Mr. Clemens).

The Garlock House, home of Olin J. Garlock, a nineteenth-century industrialist who founded Palmyra's largest industry (today it makes gaskets and seals), is an embellished white colonial, now a restaurant, at Main and Clinton streets. For those who like wry with their rye, there's a drinking establishment on Market Street, just up from Sybil Phelps's home, called The Place, apparently an irreverent take-off on Brigham Young's comment ("This is the place") when he reached the Salt Lake.

Palmyra seems not entirely comfortable with its Mormon heritage: the Historical Society Museum barely mentions it. A waggish local merchant said of the Mormons who flock here every summer: "They bring the Ten Commandments and a ten dollar bill and never break either one."

Which brings us to Joseph Smith. Palmyra prospered even before the canal opened to local commerce in 1822. A stream of immigrants from Vermont, among them a family named Smith, arrived in the bustling village. The Smiths were farmers, and a son, Joseph, when he wasn't climbing the drumlins, evinced a talent for speaking and an interest in necromancy. (The Smith homestead is owned by the Mormon church and open to the public every day. It's on Stafford Road, off State 21 south of the village.)

One September night in 1823 an angel named Moroni appeared to Joseph. The Angel Moroni directed the young man to the west side of a glacial drumlin called Cumorah, where he found a stone box and inside it a series of gold plates on which were inscribed the history of the lost tribes of the American continent. At Moroni's request, Joseph reappeared—same time, same place—each year over the next quadrennium, until in 1827 he removed the tablets and took them home. It took Joseph years of diligent labor to translate the book into English. When he was done, he and a friend lugged the tablets back up Cumorah, where they buried them in a large room in the middle of the hill. They published the translation, and thus was born the Church of Jesus Christ of Latter-day Saints, better known as the Mormons.

Cumorah was the scene in the Book of Mormon of the epic battle between the Lamanites and the Nephites, and here, on dusky evenings each July, hundreds of thousands of the Mormon faithful and curious gentiles gather to witness one of the great religious spectacles of the world, the Hill Cumorah Pageant. On the very hillside on which the dreamy Smith boy found the gold tablets, upwards of 600 Latter-day Saints—garbed in the dress of a civilization whose very existence is a matter of religious faith—act out the events told in the Book of Mormon, including the appearance of Jesus Christ on the North American continent.

Since its start in 1935, the Hill Cumorah Pageant has grown into a spectacular display of sight and sound upon a seven-level stage—an Andrew Lloyd Webber play for Mormons. (Yes, the Mormon Tabernacle Choir sings the sound track.) But the pageant is not only for the faithful; thousands of nonbelievers attend for the theater. Whatever proselytizing goes on is low-key; indeed, given time, the cute and cheery Mormon girls who directed me to the men's room could've made this gentile a convert. "I want you to know," said one of the girls, "that I *know* that all these stories you're going to see tonight are true, and reading the Book of Mormon has brought me more joy than I ever imagined." And that testament was the extent of the personal witness (or pressure) I experienced.

The Hill Cumorah Pageant takes place over a week and a half in mid-July. Admission is free, and so is parking. Bring a blanket and lawn chairs, and expect a crowd of about 30,000. The Hill is on State 21, four miles south of Palmyra and two miles north of thruway Exit 43. Take time to note the stately homes lining State 21 on the village's verge.

For festively secular fun, the Wayne County Fair is held every August on the fairgrounds on Jackson Street. This is the oldest annual fair in New York, the first one took place in 1856. Today it features a midway, harness racing, a demolition derby, and talent contests for local entertainers.

Fairs and carnivals are ubiquitous in upstate New York from June until August. They're usually auspicated by a parade, a great clamor of high-school bands, and fife and drum clubs playing with bombast and enthusiasm at wildly varying skill levels. There are Ferris wheels and merry-go-rounds and maybe even a nauseating ride like the Scrambler, but the real fun comes from just walking around. Watch the little tykes playing "I Got It," a popular Bingo-like game in which you toss rubber balls into a grid. Plunk down a quarter and try it. Then play one of the legal games of chance: you haven't a snowball's chance in Las Vegas of winning, but it's for a good cause. Write it off as a charitable contribution on your Form 1040. Next drop by the beer tent for a Genesee. Old acquaintances are renewed on summer eves over a few Gennies in beer tents from Niagara Falls to Wappingers Falls; listen in on a conversation or two and experience—vicariously—the human comedy as it plays out in 1990s upstate New York. The whole town turns out for these fairs: the owner of the canning factory is there, and so is his accountant, and so are the men and women who toil in the fields or on the assembly line. I won't go so far as to say it's the American democratic spirit in action—the owner probably isn't buying the third-shift janitor a beer—but it's as close as we ever come anymore.

Mormon visitors—indeed, all visitors to the area—may want to make a side trip ten miles to the west to the Valentown Museum and Country Store, right across from the capacious and comprehensive Eastview Shopping Mall off State 96. The gorgeous 1842 cobblestone house just before Valentown was the residence of Sarah Hall Bonesteele, the rugmaker featured in the Alling Coverlet Museum.

The Valentown Museum consists of the private collection of one of the grand old men of upstate, J. Sheldon Fisher, an octogenarian whose family name honors the nearby town of Fishers.

J. Sheldon Fisher has been an archeologist, a historian, founder of a fire company, and a staunch defender of Indian land rights at a time when New York State was swiping ancestral lands left and right. The Senecas dubbed him "He Who Collects Knowledge," and the fruits of that collection are on display at the Valentown Museum. In 1940 Mr. Fisher bought the building, a marketplace which had been designed and constructed by Levi Valentine in 1879; his purchase saved it from the wrecker's ball.

Visitors get a guided tour by Mr. Fisher himself, who fair

bubbles with enthusiasm as he walks you through two floors chockablock with Mormon artifacts, pioneer bathtubs, patent medicine bottles, and thousands of shoes and hats and knickers and other accoutrements of nineteenth-century living in this corner of the world. A bakery, a school of music, a grocery store, a cobbler's shop; the museum contains recreations of many of the stores that filled this old frame building a century ago. Contemporary craftsmen sell their wares on the bottom two floors.

Mormons making the trek to Palmyra often stop in and see Mr. Fisher. He did pathbreaking excavation work several years ago, and though he sold most of his discoveries to church historians in Salt Lake City, he retains a storehouse of knowledge about the earliest Mormons—and he also kept a chair made circa 1830 by a young furnituremaker named Brigham Young.

Araminta Jerrold, the spunky heroine of Mr. Adams' *Canal Town* (and a mighty poor speller), wrote in her diary: "Palmyra is a very Hospittible Place but not nessarily to Strangers."

Miss Jerrold's observation was made in 1820; this wanderer found it most "Hospittible" in 1993.

Take one last look at the canal as you pull out of Palmyra onto our state and interstate highway system, a public work that is impressive but lacks the brute majesty of the Erie Canal. Let the verses of one of the most popular canal songs ring in your ears:

> *Canaller, canaller*
> *You son of a bitch*
> *You'll die on the towpath*
> *You'll be buried in the ditch*
> *Canaller, canaller*
> *You work on Sunday*
> *You'll never get rich*

Then disappear into the drumlins and listen for an angel's whisper.

Hill Cumorah Pageant, 315-597-6808
Historic Palmyra (all non-Mormon museums), 315-597-6981
Grandin Building and Joseph Smith House, 315-597-0019
Palmyra Chamber of Commerce, 315-597-5663
Valentown Museum and Country Store, 716-924-2645

2

Kinderhook

From New York City, take the Taconic State Parkway north, exit at State 23, drive west for five miles, then take State 9H north for ten miles. From the north or west, take Exit 21A of the New York State Thruway, go east on I-90 for seven miles, then take State 9H south for twelve more.

This is Dutch New York, where the patroons usually had surnames beginning with "Van." Later waves of immigration overwhelmed the Hollanders—the old finger in the dike dilemma—but Van Buren and Van Tassel are still the biggest names in town, even though one is dead and the other lives only in the undying pages of fiction.

Martin Van Buren, eighth president of the United States, lived just outside Kinderhook on an estate he named Lindenwald after the linden trees that cover the property. Lindenwald is a mishmash of architectural styles (Gothic, Federal, Victorian, Italianate) that has been often mocked but remains impressive, especially to those of us with a taste for enthusiastic eclecticism. It is imposing and forlorn, sitting amidst twenty-two acres, and it's not hard to feel sorry for Matty the ex-president, scheming in this magnificent isolation and waiting for the young disciples and wisdom-seekers who never came.

Kinderhook

Martin Van Buren was a tavernkeeper's son, born in Kinderhook in 1782. (As such he was the first president who was born a citizen of the sovereign United States.) His father's establishment doubled as a polling place on election day, so Matty was born to the electioneering business. He grew into an ambitious young lawyer whose political acumen attracted the attention and sponsorship of the rakish Aaron Burr—Matty's real father, scurrilous rumor always had it. (Burr stayed at the family tavern, you see, and Matty's mother was toothsome, and Burr was a rake of legendary appetites.)

Van Buren mastered New York politics; from surrogate of Columbia County he went on to the state senate, then state attorney general, and in 1821 he was elected a United States senator, whereupon he set about creating the Democratic party, using as its linchpin a Tennessee war hero of strong passions named Andrew Jackson. They were an odd couple: Van Buren the brilliant if bland strategist, and Jackson the simple and sanguine westerner. In 1832, after Vice President John C. Calhoun had run afoul of President Jackson, Old Hickory enlisted Van Buren as his (successful) running mate. Four years later, the tavernkeeper's boy was elected president.

Van Buren succeeded Jackson to the presidency but he never won a place in his countrymen's hearts. The depression of 1837 knocked him off stride, and the sectional conflicts on which Jackson had successfully kept a lid started to boil over. He was defeated in 1840 by William Henry Harrison, an aristocrat who ran as the incarnation of log cabins and hard cider. Harrison, the Virginia squire, posed as a man of the people—a Whiggish Andy Jackson—while Van Buren, the authentic populist, the striving son of a taproom operator, was tagged as a foppish dandy and "Van Van, the used-up man."

He was hardly used up. Van Buren returned to Kinderhook and in 1841 he bought the only home he ever owned—Lindenwald, a classic upstate Federal-style home built in 1797. His was not a golfing and loafing retirement. Van Buren kept his fingers in several political pies, even running for president again in 1848 on the

Free-Soil ticket, a fascinating alliance of antislavery Whigs and northern laissez-faire Democrats. He was clobbered, but it was a noble effort.

Lindenwald was intended to be a Monticello, a Hermitage, a grand manorial home to a beloved ex-president who would receive well-wishers, foreign dignitaries, and the political cognoscenti. In 1849 Van Buren's son Smith and architect Richard Upjohn modified—others say adulterated, defaced, trashed—Lindenwald with extensive renovations and redecorating that today wouldn't exactly pass muster with Martha Stewart. The old red-brick farmhouse was expanded and embroidered till it was scarcely recognizable. Walls were plastered over, its eighteen rooms were doubled to thirty-six. A controversial Italian pagoda was added. The tasteful scoffed—Matty himself was bemused by some of the changes—

Lindenwald, home of President Martin Van Buren

and Lindenwald later became, among other things, a sanitarium and antique store before the National Park Service acquired it in 1974.

"When legend becomes fact, print the legend," the cynical newspaperman cracked in John Ford's elegiac western *The Man Who Shot Liberty Valance.* Similarly, as part of our policy of crediting local legends in a, well, credulous manner, the slang word *okay* is derived from "Old Kinderhook," a Van Buren nickname which itself came from the inscription on crates of apples from the town. Probably. Gregg Berninger, our knowledgeable guide, claimed that on average, each American says *okay* seven times a day.

Van Buren got a bad rap as a trimmer, a wily politico wedded to intrigue and equivocation. *Vanburenish*, a deprecatory adjective of the nineteenth century, meant one who is unwilling to take a stand. Foes (and even some uneasy friends) called him "the Little Magician" and "the Red Fox of Kinderhook." Ranger Berninger made a spirited defense of Matty and I, for one, wholeheartedly concur. (Those in search of fortifying history to prepare them for Lindenwald may want to read John Niven's *Martin Van Buren: The Romantic Age of American Politics* or Robert Remini's *Martin Van Buren and The Making of The Democratic Party.*)

Lindenwald is open seven days a week from May to October; the price of admission is very modest. About half the items in the home are Van Buren's; the rest are of his era. There are special events throughout the nonwinter seasons; actors impersonating various presidents make occasional appearances. (Frank Cappozzi, a ranger at the park and one of the performers, is a dead ringer for Jason Robards. But can he act?) Lindenwald goes dark after the requiem held on December 5, the president's birthday.

The mourners—a handful, usually, for Matty was not Abe and Kinderhook is not Springfield—assemble at the Kinderhook Reformed Church Cemetery on Albany Avenue, one mile west of the village center. The Van Buren family shaft is suitably modest, and even if you follow the signs it'll take a few minutes to locate it. Like the other Hudson Valley president with a Dutch name, Martin Van Buren was born and buried in the same town, and if Kinderhook hasn't the same cachet as Hyde Park, that says more about us than poor Van.

Martin Van Buren had met Washington Irving in 1831, when the celebrated writer was serving in a patronage post in England. They became lifelong friends, sharing genteely radical Democratic politics, and Irving turned down Matty's offer in 1838 to be secretary of the navy (the post went to another Hudson Valley writer, James Kirke Paulding).

Irving wrote *The Legend of Sleepy Hollow* while staying at Lindenwald, though not as a guest of Van Buren. The Knickerbocker chronicler had been a tutor for the children of Judge Peter Van Ness, a previous owner, and while in residence he gobbled up local color the way Ichabod Crane wolfed down sweetmeats.

Irving set his tale in Tarrytown but peopled it with Kinderhookers. Ichabod Crane, the lanky pedantic Yankee know-it-all, was based on an oddball local schoolmaster named Jesse Merwin. The beautiful and coquettish Katrina Van Tassel, apple of Ichabod's eye, had her real-life counterpart in Helen Van Alen. Brom Bones, the "roystering blade" who gave Ichabod his comeuppance and won Katrina's heart, has no known Kinderhook correspondent.

The blooming Katrina was the daughter of "a substantial Dutch farmer" whose home you can visit just one mile north of Lindenwald on State 9H. The Luykas Van Alen home is a 1737 two-story farmhouse and monument to our Dutch agriculturalist forefathers.

Each of the three first-floor rooms has a Dutch fireplace, jambless and bordered by Dutch tiles. Before you visit, read Irving's lovingly detailed description of the Van Tassel's sumptuous dinner table. (My wife always asks me to skip this part when we read the story aloud each Halloween.) I won't say you can almost smell the doughnuts and crullers and pumpkin pies, but the more imaginative may work up an appetite.

The second floor, now used for storage, contains one of our favorite finds, a "senility crate" in which doddering dotard Dutchmen were kept. Though designed, I'm sure, with the best intentions, the senility crate must've been a mighty incentive to oldsters to quit whining about their aches and pains.

Also on the property is the Ichabod Crane Schoolhouse, a fanciful name for a nineteenth-century readin' and writin' center of the one-room variety.

Guided tours of the Van Alen House are offered from Memorial Day to Labor Day except on Tuesdays. A five-dollar admission fee gets you in the Van Alen House and the Vanderpoel House, to which we'll get presently. An antique show and eighteenth-century fair are held on the grounds each summer. Movie-goers may experience the shock of recognition: the Van Alen House appears in Martin Scorsese's film of Edith Wharton's *The Age of Innocence*.

From State 9H, take Hudson Street back into the village. You'll pass Martin Van Buren's birthsite (gone with the wind, designated by a marker) on the left, as well as St. Paul's Episcopal Church, a noteworthy example of "board and batten" Gothic architecture. St. Paul's was a charity job by architect Richard Upjohn, the Frankenstein—or ingenious renovator—of Lindenwald.

The James Vanderpoel House, at 16 Broad Street, is a circa-1820 Federal-style home that was the residence of an eminent local attorney and friend of Van Buren's. (The Vanderpoels' daughter married John Van Buren.) The gracious house can be seen as the sequel to the Van Alen House; this is how the sons and daughters of the prosperous Hudson Valley Dutch lived. Guide Connie Nooney gave us an informative tour; the curved staircase and imposing secretary are impressive. Be sure to go down to the basement to see the eighteen-inch-high figurines of a score of Kinderhook eminencies. These mannikins, made in 1929, represent such persons as Martin Van Buren, Washington Irving, and Helen Van Alen.

A large craft festival is held on the Vanderpoel grounds in June; garden clubs deck the halls of the home in December. Like the Van Alen House, the Vanderpoel House is open between Memorial Day and Labor Day except on Tuesdays.

Right around the corner, at 5 Albany Avenue, is the Columbia

County Museum. Housed in a 1916 Masonic Temple, the museum contains rotating exhibits of local history; we saw a charming group of sketches and photos of distinguished buildings done by schoolchildren. (The Second Empire home just two doors south of the Vanderpoel House was a favorite subject.) The museum is open year-round on weekdays and on weekends from Memorial Day to Labor Day.

Kinderhook's kids are to be envied or pitied; they attend Ichabod Crane High School, whose nickname is the Riders and whose mascot is a headless horseman. This seemed wonderfully quaint to us, though Connie Nooney at the Vanderpoel House pointed out that the prospect of playing a team called Ichabod Crane doesn't exactly strike fear into the hearts of opposing athletes. The district has no football team, which is probably just as well.

There is a delicious irony in the name. Ichabod Crane was a terrible teacher! He was a Connecticut nitwit who beat his charges with the ferule and swore by the truth of Cotton Mather's History of *New England Witchcraft*. He was a fool and a coward; his sole virtue was an appreciation of good food.

Crane would've tarried long in modern Kinderhook, sponging meals. Route 9 is dotted with fruit stands and pick-your-own strawberry fields and apple orchards. Brosen's Farm Stand and Golden Harvest Farms lie just north of town on State 9; the latter will press your apples into cider.

And if you should visit Kinderhook some crisp fall evening— say, the night of October 31—give goblins on horseback the right-of-way, and avoid round orange projectiles.

18

Brosen's Farm Stand, 518-758-9292
Columbia County Museum/James Vanderpoel House/Luykas Van
   Alen House, 518-758-9265
Columbia County Tourism, 518-828-3375
Lindenwald (Martin Van Buren National Historic Site),
   518-758-9689

3

Le Roy

Get off the New York State Thruway at Exit 47, then take State 19 south for three miles. Or take State 5, an old Indian trail, until it becomes Main Street, Le Roy. (Le Roy itself was once a Seneca Indian campsite.)

For a town built on Jell-O, Le Roy has an admirable solidity. The *Buffalo Illustrated Times* called it "one of the handsomest towns in the whole state" in 1905, and the boom times experienced shortly thereafter left pleasing and distinguished marks and monuments that stand to this day.

The gelatin dessert was perfected, if not invented, by a Le Roy carpenter named Pearl Bixby Wait, who lacked the means to market his brainchild and sold it in 1899 to a patent medicine businessman named Orator Woodward for $450. (The first patent for a jelly made with water was granted in 1845 to Peter Cooper, later the Greenback party candidate for president in 1876. And Greenbacks are exactly what this concoction made, in spades, though not for Cooper or Wait.)

After seven years of aggressive and inventive marketing, Jell-O sales topped the million-dollar mark, and from there, under the direction of Orator's son Ernest, they zoomed ever upward. Pearl Wait lived on West Main Street. He died in 1915 at the age of forty-two, and he must have been tortured by what-might-have-beens for all of his too-brief life.

Le Roy has its own version of the "urban legends"—alligators in sewers, rats fried in fast-food chicken—that titillate Americans. They have to do with the huge vats of Jell-O that workers, well, *modified* in the plant, and you're probably better off not knowing the details.

The Woodwards were paternalistic, with all the good and bad things that implies. The family paid the hospital bills of its personal employees; my grandfather was a handyman around the estate, so my mother's birthing was paid for by the Jell-O eaters of America. (Thank you, by the way.)

To gaze upon the old Jell-O plant just drive up North Street for half a mile. See the low red-brick factory on the left-hand side? That's where the lime Jell-O salad your mom served was born.

Jell-O, by then owned by General Foods, pulled out of Le Roy in 1964. A container company and an evangelical church occupy the building today, though it was vacant for quite some years, and Le Roy suffered in its absence. Fittingly, the bosky Macpelah cemetery abuts the plant. The Woodward plot is prominent. Despite its misfortune, you can't keep a good town down, and Le Roy has rebounded nicely from Jell-O's desertion.

Park on Wolcott Street, along the Oatka Creek, which meanders through town, bisecting Main Street. The creek borders the pretty campus of Le Roy Central School. The vista from downtown creekside is soothing and placid. Loll around on the grass and watch the anglers fish for perch and bass; across the creek, under the bridge, are the remains of Herman Le Roy's gristmill, built in 1803.

The village of Le Roy stages the Oatka Festival every July on these grounds: crafts and antiques and sausages are sold; speeches are declaimed; a parade marches on. One year an old-timers game was played between the graying veterans of the Le Roy and neighboring Lime Rock town baseball teams of the 1940s. The bragging rights that went to the victors were once much prized; my older relatives, the northern Italians who settled Lime Rock at the turn of the century, still talk about the raucous celebrations in the tiny hamlet whenever their nine defeated the smug cosmopolites of Le Roy.

Wolcott turns into Church Street; the second edifice down Church, the two-and-a-half-story brick building overlooking the Oatka, was the home of the S. C. Wells Company, maker of magic elixirs to cure all ills, real and imagined. Le Roy was a veritable Detroit of patent medicines: Pope's Blood and Liver Medicine, Mother Gray's Sweet Powders for Children, Allen's Discovery for Piles, and Rough on Bile Pills were among the curatives produced by several manufactories in Le Roy. Orator Woodward himself, before becoming the king of Jell-O, made and peddled Racoon Corn Plasters, Grain-O, and other such medicinal wonders.

Churches impart a sacred tint to this Main Street tableau. The Presbyterian dates from 1826; St. Mark's Episcopal, made of locally mined limestone, from 1869; the First Baptist Church, a melange of styles, was erected in the 1820s; the United Methodist Church was constructed in 1886. The Methodists almost tore their temple down recently, but after a bitter fight the church was saved and the pastor left for less preservationist-minded pastures. The Methodist church contains a pipe organ donated by Cora T. Woodward in 1917; it is magnificent, so push at the doors and see if they admit entrance. Down the street in a westerly direction the Lovria Memorial Chapel, a Second Empire–style residence built in the 1870s and now a funeral home, is a somber and dignified presence.

Scribble out a postcard and stop in the post office just over the bridge. A joint project of the Woodwards and the New Deal, the building has a limestone exterior and a cupola with an illuminated clock. Inside are gray marble wainscoting and black and white checkerboard terrazzo floors. Walk two blocks west and you'll come to the Village Hall, designed by the renowned Rochester architect and writer Claude Bragdon.

Once you've taken the town's measure, visit the Le Roy House at 23 East Main Street. Constructed in 1817, the edifice served as a land office in its infancy and is now a fine museum of local history, open from 10:00 A.M. to 4:00 P.M. through Friday. No admission fee is charged.

The Le Roy House has an impressive collection of Jell-O memorabilia, Victorian furniture and dress, and all manner of Le Roy collectibles. It takes an hour or so to tour the museum, and the volunteer docents are helpful. They know and love Le Roy, and if you enjoy gossip about the long dead, they'll give you the lowdown on their town.

The Le Roy House contains a beautifully executed painting of the village in its early years by Emma Keeney Bixby, Ingham University Class of 1845. This school educated 8,000 young women between 1837 and its demise in 1892. It is but a memory now on the site upon which Le Roy High School sits. The Woodward Memorial Library, a Classical Revival structure, was built in 1930 using stone from Ingham. (An Ingham chancellor, the Reverend Samuel Burchard, was the impolitic clergyman who maligned the Democrats as the party of "rum, Romanism, and rebellion," thus dealing the fatal blow to his candidate, Republican James G. Blaine, "the Plumed Knight," in the 1884 presidential election.)

Walk east on maple-lined Main Street, past a long row of stately homes; see how nicely they have settled, despite their gelatinous foundations.

The last house on the left before the golf course was built by Donald Woodward in 1929. Across the street, atop a hill looking down upon a rambling greensward, is Mercy Grove, a Woodward estate which was later donated to a religious order.

Le Roy's commercial Main Street is a bit down at the heels, but walk it anyway. Stop in for a Genny draft at the Eagle, where topers have been tipping them back since 1825. (The Reverend Burchard, no doubt, disapproved.) A family friend of prodigious thirst used to sit at a stool all day and cadge beers from walk-ins: he is gone, RIP, but not forgotten, so bring an extra seventy-five cents and buy a brew for the old man at the end of the bar. Tell him it's on Joe.

Across the street is a tavern of even hoarier vintage: the

Wiss, erected in 1802. When last we checked, potent libations were still being served in cold glasses.

Le Roy has several fine restaurants: the fare is hearty and American, the ambiance unself-consciously small-town. One distinguished eatery, the D & R Depot on Lake Street, resides in a refurbished rectangular brick station built in 1901 by the Buffalo, Rochester, and Pittsburgh Railroad. Pictures of the mostly Irish and Italian men who built and ran the railroad dot the walls; period music whispers from the loudspeaker from which dispatchers once cried, "All aboard for Church-ville, Rah-chester, Sara-cuse, U-tica . . ." The effect is pleasantly anachronistic and the food is good.

If you visit Le Roy in the fall, drive north on State 19 for a mile, then take a right onto the Oatka Trail. The yellow, orange, and auburn leaves garland the trees, arching over the road like a canopy and giving the impression that you're traveling through an arboreal tunnel. The McPherson family has owned an apple orchard on the trail since about 1800. Stop by for a bag of Macs and a jug of apple cider.

Genesee is the most heavily agricultural county in western New York; the land is flat and fertile and splendidly verdant in springtime. A Le Royan, Calvin Keeney, developed the first stringless bean: "He is the man who took the string out of the bean," eulogized one admirer. Order an edible pod at a local eatery and think of Calvin, who in the midnineteenth century lived in the imposing residence at 13 West Main Street.

When you get back into town, take State 19 south for a spell until you get to Cole Road, onto which you'll turn right. Wander down the road until it intersects the Bethany–Le Roy Road; the old farmhouse on the corner, 6928 Cole Road, has an octagon outhouse in the yard. Legend has it that a swain built the outhouse for his beloved, who then jilted him. (Is it any wonder? The romantic devil!)

A rather more natural wonder can be seen out North Street, a mile and a half beyond the Jell-O plant. Where the street breaks sharply left, pull right onto the dirt road. Park the car, slip into your

24

hiking boots, and follow the gravel path for several hundred paces until you hear the . . . if not roar, like our neighbor Niagara to the west, then loud gurgle of the Buttermilk Falls of Oatka Creek. ("Buttermilk Falls" was the name of the village before the Le Roy family came to, or rather bought, the town.)

The cataracts drop seventy feet to a bubbling froth that looks almost good enough to drink, thus the name. Local artists love this scene; if you paint, bring an easel. Paths take you down to a view of the falls which deluges the senses, but be forewarned: they are steep and, in the summer, overgrown with weeds and wildflowers. If, like Woody Allen, you are at "two with nature," you're hereby advised to forget Buttermilk Falls and retire to the nearest public house.

Le Roy—a regal name if you're a Frenchman—has a snooty reputation among its neighbors, which is odd considering that its mansions and dignified tree-lined Main Street were constructed on a base of horse hooves and quack medicine. My wife has urged me to use, as an epigraph to a book on the literature of New York, the Elton John line, "Some things look better, baby/Just passing through," and I've always wondered if that doesn't fit Le Roy to a T. It is picturesque and lazy, and it looks as if Norman Rockwell drew it, yet its school has for years had a reputation for rowdiness. I'm not discouraging a visit: indeed, I've chosen Le Roy from among the hundreds of country towns eligible for inclusion in this book. Le Roy is pretty to look at and I have relatives, native to the town, who love it dearly. I'm just suggesting that sometimes the gap between appearance and reality is canyonesque.

Drive east on State 5 just past the golf course and take a left onto Flint Hill Road. Follow its curves for a couple of miles and you'll come to the Genesee Country Village, a reconstructed nineteenth century village that is Upstate's Williamsburg.

The village began as the dream of John L. ("Jack") Wehle of the Genesee Brewing family. (You must, of course, drink Genny when visiting local watering holes.) From modest beginnings in 1966, the Genesee Country Village has acquired—and moved, piece by piece, and lovingly restored—some fifty-seven regional buildings of diverse, even breathtaking architecture. Many of these homes and shops were in states of extreme disrepair before the museum rescued them.

There is an octagon house, a curiosity dating from 1870. The visionary—though some thought him bats—who fought valiantly to popularize the eight-sided home was a local boy, Orson Fowler of Cohocton, who lectured tirelessly on the functional disadvantages of the mere four-sided home. (They make better use of space, and the devil can never corner you within an octagon.) Fowler was also a high priest in the queer pseudo-science of phrenology, which held that a man's character can be deduced by analyzing the shape of his skull.

The village's two hundred acres include a general store, a

The Octagon House at the Genesee Country Museum

seminary, a variety of homes (including the Greek Revival in which the region's greatest industrialist, George Eastman, was born), a pharmacy, a tavern (sorry, no grog), a Quaker meetinghouse, Methodist and Roman Catholic churches, an insurance office, and shops and barns in which cobblers, blacksmiths, tinsmiths, potters, printers, and other craftsmen and women practice their trades.

Docents are posted in each building, wearing period dress, but there is nothing hokey or staged about the village. These are people recreating the lives of their forbearers in a spirit of reverence dashed with fun. Special events are scheduled throughout the season, which runs from early May until mid-October. Pioneer-game days for the kids, Civil War encampment reenactments, and a grand Fourth of July celebration are highlights. Weddings are sometimes held in the chapel; call ahead and really surprise your beloved.

The admission is a bit steep—$10 for adults, and a sliding scale for children and older folks as I write this in the fall of 1993—but it's just a couple of bucks more than you'd pay to watch *Police Academy VII* at the local cinema, so dig deep and enjoy.

And don't miss the John L. Wehle Gallery of Sporting Art appended to the village. It features one of the largest collections of wildlife art in America and includes paintings, sculptures, and prints by the likes of Frederic Remington, Antoine-Louis Barye, W. R. Leigh, and a local artist, the late Roy M. Mason of nearby Batavia, who has been twinned by more than one critic with Winslow Homer.

I can't leave Le Roy without mentioning my hometown, Batavia, a city of 16,000 ten miles to the west on State 5. Once a busy industrial city, Batavia committed municipal suicide in the 1960s when it, like so many small upstate cities, bought into the federal government's urban renewal program. The brick storefronts and walkups teeming with life were razed; a sterile mall was built upon the ruins, and we have yet to resuscitate. Nevertheless, if you're in Le Roy you may as well scoot over to Batavia. Some fine shops remain, and sprinkled here and there are outstanding buildings (Richmond Memorial Library, Genesee County Sheriff's

Office, the Holland Land Office Museum, and the homes along broad old Ellicott Avenue) which serve as the remnant, reminding us of the city our forefathers and mothers built and that we, their ungrateful prodigals, tore down. Let Batavia serve as a caution to all who place progress above the humane values.

D & R Depot, 716-768-6270
Genesee County Chamber of Commerce, 800-622-2686
Genesee Country Village, 716-538-6822
Le Roy House, 716-768-7433
Village of Le Roy (Oatka Festival), 716-768-2140

4

Cooperstown

Take the New York State Thruway to Exit 30, then drive State 28 south for twenty-five miles. From New York City, take thruway Exit 21 (Catskill), then State routes 23 west, 145 north, US 20 west, and State 80 south.

Cooperstown, home of America's first internationally recognized novelist, is today the most famous small town in New York—for reasons that have nothing whatsoever to do with James Fenimore Cooper and his frontier fictions.

The Coopers settled on the shore of Otsego Lake in 1790. William Cooper bought 100,000 acres of land, promptly becoming the laird of the county and eponym of the town. He was a judge, a man of strong passions and prejudices, and he died in 1809 of complications from an assault by a political foe.

The Judge's son James became the most popular novelist of the early American republic. He set many of his tales in his father's demesne, and he sometimes called the lake "Glimmerglass" in his fiction. After sojourns at sea, in Europe, and downstate in Westchester County, James returned to Cooperstown in 1834.

Reverence for the prodigal revenant dissipated like the morning dew. James forbade his neighbors to picnic on his property, and despite his Jacksonian political sympathies he played the lord of the manor to the hilt. (Three Mile Point, the scenic spot from which James kicked out the canaille, is three miles north of Cooperstown on State 80.)

In a way, Cooper's reputation never recovered from a vicious but funny essay by Mark Twain in which Twain noted that Cooper had committed 114 literary offenses out of a possible 115. But guess who's having the last laugh: a Cooper revival flared in the early 1990s with the success of the latest film version of *Last of the Mohicans*. Directed by "Miami Vice" creator Michael Mann, the movie flew by at breakneck pace; there were no pastels but Natty Bumppo looked an awful lot like Don Johnson in buckskin. That same year, a remake of *The Adventures of Huckleberry Finn* flopped—like so many of Mr. Clemens's business ventures.

James Fenimore Cooper died in 1851 and was buried in the family plot in Christ Church Cemetery. A Leatherstocking monument—twenty-five feet high, surmounted by the Indian hunter and his trusty dog—is on the eastern shore of Otsego Lake.

A later Cooperstown family, the Clarks, grew rich upon Singer sewing machines. Edward Clark, progenitor of the fortune, built a miniature castle called Kingfisher Tower on a promontory jutting out into the Otsego. He somewhat pompously averred that it gave "a character of antiquity to the lake," though it can only be appreciated by those "whose minds can rise above simple notions of utility to an appreciation of art joined to nature." Even the basest philistines can see Kingfisher: it's off County 31, about three miles north of town.

A descendant, Stephen C. Clark, a man of practically philanthropic bent, was the impetus behind the creation of the three museums that have made Cooperstown one of the favorite tourist spots in the east: the Farmers' Museum, the Fenimore House, and the granddaddy of sporting reliquaries, the National Baseball Hall of Fame.

The Farmers' Museum, founded in 1943 on the vast Clark acreage on State 80, is a wonderful sprawling collection of tools, implements, and transplanted buildings that serve as a living

Kingfisher Tower on Lake Otsego

memorial to rural New York's past. Don't misunderstand: this is no tedious batch of adzes and axes arranged in a musty setting. The epigraph over the barn door entrance to the Exhibition Center states the museum's purpose:

> *To show how the plain people of*
> *yesterday, in doing their daily work,*
> *built a great nation, where only a*
> *great forest had stood.*

They did so with heart and muscle and faith—and machinery. In the Textile Loft you can watch craftswomen turn flax into cloth on vintage spinning wheels and looms, and learn all about the origin of "Pop! Goes the Weasel" to boot. Broommakers, woodworkers, and others ply their trades in the midst of an enormous collection of nineteenth-century artifacts.

Our favorite exhibit is the one, the only, the original Cardiff Giant, basis for one of the great hoaxes in American history. The giant—2,990 pounds of what seems to be chalky petrified bone, lips curved in beatific contentment—was unearthed from farmland in nearby Cardiff in 1869. Stub Newell, the farmer, invited the locals over for a look-see, and before long a stream of visitors, many of them estimable geologists and archeologists, invaded Cardiff. A Harvard scholar claimed to find Phoenician scrawlings on the underarm; he translated them to "Tamur, god of gods," and speculated that the giant was a totem left behind by ancient explorers.

Newell turned down P. T. Barnum's offer of $150,000 and took the giant on tour himself, raking in the dough. But then a skeptical academic, Professor O. C. Marsh, discovered that an Iowan had made the giant out of gypsum. Stub confessed to the hoax, a coven of know-it-alls ate crow, and, according to folk historian Carl Carmer, "Stub's giant got more popular than ever." Today he rests comfortably in the haymow of the Exhibition Center.

Leave the barn and amble out into the Village Crossroads. This is what Main Street looked like in a thriving upstate town of the 1840s. There is a schoolhouse, a tavern, a church, a pharmacy— eleven buildings in all. Printers, blacksmiths, and cooks do their respective things, all the while fielding questions from visitors. (Many of the products are for sale in the gift shop.)

The Farmers' Museum is open from April until December. A variety of special events are scheduled throughout the season, including sleigh rides and an Independence Day bash worthy of upstate, a hotbed of secessional patriotism in 1776. Admission is a tad pricey (meaning, in this area, over $5); your best bet is to buy a combination ticket gaining you entrance to the Farmers' Museum, Fenimore House, and the Baseball Hall of Fame. At press time these sold for $13 for adults and $5 for children aged seven to fifteen. (Tykes pay nothing.)

Across the street from the Farmers' Museum is the stone Fenimore House, which Edward S. Clark constructed in 1932. The handsome smaller building next door is the library of the New York State Historical Association, which has done so much to keep the flame lit in our sometimes forgetful and forgotten region. (Speaking of fire, the Cooper manse burned to the ground in 1853.)

The Fenimore House is a must for anyone who loves American art, and in particular the Hudson River school of landscape painters. Thomas Cole's epic *Last of the Mohicans*, William Sidney Mount's *Ringing the Pig*, Gilbert Stuart's *Joseph Brandt*, the portraits of the talented itinerant Noah North, and a dazzlingly rich variety of folk art, from weather vanes to cigar store Indians, are displayed in the Fenimore House. Prints and postcards amply demonstrating the "Yorker" artistic genius are on sale at the excellent bookstore on the first floor.

The second floor contains the Hall of Life Masks: twenty-two busts made by John H. I. Browere from facial moldings taken of Thomas Jefferson, Henry Clay, Dolley Madison, and other celebrities (and rogues) of the Era of Good Feelings. The busts are eerily alive, and the paucity of spectators in the Hall of Life Masks contrasts sharply with the crowds that assemble in the Baseball Hall of Fame just down the road. But then John Adams never could hit the slider.

Okay, so maybe a West Point cadet named Abner Doubleday didn't invent baseball in Cooperstown in the summer of 1839, but

Farmers' Museum at Cooperstown

the legend begat the Baseball Hall of Fame, which since its grand opening on June 12, 1939 has become the most popular sports museum in America, if not the world. More than 400,000 people pass through its doors annually, no mean feat considering just how out-of-the-way Cooperstown is.

(Almost all of these pilgrims come in cars. The Hall of Fame is on Main Street. The town's population is barely 2,000. Add these facts up and you'll understand why Cooperstownies want you to park in one of three park-and-ride lots on State routes 80 and 28 and hop the free trolley into town. Otherwise be content with parking on a side street and walking.)

The centerpiece of this shrine is the Hall of Fame Gallery, with its plaques honoring the more than 200 men—or "immortals," as the baseball scribe had it—who have been elected to membership. No, Shoeless Joe Jackson hasn't a plaque, nor does Pete Rose—yet. The kids tend to be less awed than Dad by seeing Wee Willie Keeler in bronze; they'd sooner see Abbott and Costello doing "Who's on First?" on video monitors, or sit in the bleacher-like 200-seat auditorium and watch baseball movies. As with most large museums, the real pleasure is found in its nooks and crannies where you can see George Brett's infamous pine tar-covered bat, or hear the voice of Babe Ruth on a scratchy tape.

The jerseyed hordes descend on Cooper's bonnie burg for the Hall of Fame induction ceremony in the dog days of summer. An exhibition baseball game between two major league clubs is played the next day at Doubleday Stadium on Susquehanna Avenue. Traffic is a killer on induction weekend, especially if a Yankee has snuck into the pantheon—the gridlock alone is reason enough to keep Phil Rizzuto out of the Hall—but what ardent fan can pass up the chance to rub shoulders (or at least spot through binoculars) Willie Mays, Stan Musial, Ted Williams, and a virtual galaxy of the American game's most fulgurant stars. Autograph sessions—for a price, naturally; the bucolic game long ago reached the end of innocence—are common on mecca weekend.

The Hall of Fame is open every day but Thanksgiving, Christmas, and New Year's Day.

Visit the most popular sports museum in the world

You may want to test your mettle at the Doubleday Batting Range adjacent to Doubleday Stadium. Grab a bat and stride to the plate like Roy Hobbs, where you can whiff at seventeen different pitches—including a right-hand curve that has fantasy leaguers bailing out faster than a mate in a waterlogged lifeboat. A radar gun clocks your own pitches; hurl a fastball with all your might, invert the measured speed of 66 MPH to 99 MPH, and call yourself Nolan Ryan. (The Chamber of Commerce Visitor's Information Center is just a weak pop fly away, in Higgins Cottage, an 1856 Greek Revival.)

Cooperstown

Cooperstown's busy downtown is filled with baseball memorabilia and autograph shops. (Hint: if you see a Honus Wagner card for five dollars, buy it.) The Larry Fritsch Baseball Card Museum at 10 Chestnut Street, open seven days a week, contains 20,000 of the rarest of the more than one million items Mr. Fritsch accumulated in a half century of collecting. Highlights include "The Wagner" from the 1909–1911 American Tobacco Trust set and a 1952 Mickey Mantle. An admission fee is charged.

Artwork of a different sort is on display at the Cooperstown Art Association Galleries at 22 Main Street. Regional artists exhibit their work, as they do at The Pioneer Gallery at 55 Pioneer Street. The Pioneer is notable, too, for its location: the Smithy, a 1786 blacksmith's shop built by William Cooper. Local history exhibits occupy much of the third floor.

For those willing to forgive the rich-kid gearheads who always got the girl in high school, the Corvette Americana Hall of Fame is three miles down State 28. The thirty-plus cars—including an inaugural 1953—are posed against backdrop murals of famous American landscapes. Cult movie buffs will want to see the four-wheeled stars of *Corvette Summer* and *Death Race 2000*. An appended Americana museum features tributes to pop culture icons, among them James Dean, Marilyn Monroe, and Bruce Springsteen, scored by the music and movie sound tracks of their eras.

If you dug *Corvette Summer*, you'll really flip over the Glimmerglass Opera, several miles north of town on State 80. In just two decades Glimmerglass has emerged as American opera's summer haven; each July and August, works by the old European masters and upstart Statesiders are staged in an Arcadian setting. Ticket prices range from fourteen to fifty-two dollars.

There are so many quaint bed and breakfasts and guest houses in Cooperstown that you'll think you've died and gone to Vermont. Among larger inns, the Otesaga Hotel, an imposing lakeside resort with columns and a veranda right out of the plantation South, is a Clark family operation that is open from May to October.

The Clarks deemed tourism to be Cooperstown's ticket to

nonpolluting profit, and they deemed right, but the area is still heavily agricultural. Beginning in late August and running through the fall, the Fly Creek Cider Mill on Valley Road, three miles north of town, turns apples into cider with the aid of an 1889 Boomer and Boscher press, a 1924 John Deere Waterloo Boy tractor engine, and good old-fashioned waterpower from Fly Creek.

Cider is truly the ambrosial drink of upstate New York; oceans of this nectar are on sale at the Fly Creek Cider Mill, along with homemade jams and jellies, fudge, New York State cheeses, and harvest decorations. On the last Sunday in September the 4-H celebrates Johnny Appleseed Day, a kind of teach-in about apples, while the Applefest Weekend, in October, sponsored by the Fly Creek Methodist Church, features hayrides, magic tricks, and brownies.

Otsego Lake teems with salmon, lake trout, and the varieties of whitefish known as "Otsego bass." Anglers recommend that you fish from a boat; rentals are available up and down the eight-mile-long Glimmerglass, and a public launching site can be found on the lake's southern tip.

If you'd rather leave the navigating to others, Classic Boat Tours offers Otsego cruises from May through October on two venerable wooden craft, the *Chief Uncas* and the *Narra Mattah*.

Those who like their recreation to leave them emaciated, dehydrated, and soaked with perspiration may enter the Glimmerglass Triathlon in late September; the local chamber of commerce has the details.

On a slightly less strenuous note—and for boys only—the Cooperstown Baseball Camp offers weeklong instruction and plenty of outings throughout the summer. Campers (a maximum of twenty-six) bunk in a renovated mansion by night and play ball by day.

I can't let Cooperstown go by without mentioning the New York–Pennsylvania Baseball League, of which Otsego County's Oneonta is a charter member. The NYP is a Class A league; Oneonta is where the New York Yankees send their greenest prospects. The baseball is of high quality—these are pros, after all, however recently graduated into shaving many of them are—and the stadiums are old and intimate. Sit close enough and you can hear the manager chew out an umpire or patiently instruct an erring shortstop. There is no finer baseball anywhere on earth: skilled, enthusiastic players in a human-scale setting. You can have your Mets and Blue Jays and sulking millionaires and futuristic domed parks: long live the Oneonta Yankees and the Batavia Clippers and the Utica Blue Sox! You may be sure that each and every player has in the back of his mind an eventual trip to this little place called Cooperstown. . . .

Baseball Hall of Fame, 607-547-9988
Classic Boat Tours, 607-547-5295
Cooperstown Art Association Galleries, 607-547-9777
Cooperstown Baseball Camp, 908-277-3715
Cooperstown Chamber of Commerce, 607-547-9983
Corvette Americana Hall of Fame, 607-547-4135
Farmers' Museum, 607-547-2593
Fenimore House Museum, 607-547-2533
Fly Creek Cider Mill, 607-547-9692
Glimmerglass Opera, 607-547-5704
Larry Fritsch Baseball Card Museum, 607-547-9464
New York State Department of Environmental Conservation
        Region 4 (for fishing information), 607-652-7364
Otesaga Hotel, 607-547-9931
Otsego County Chamber of Commerce, 607-432-4500
Pioneer Galley, 607-547-8671

5

East Aurora

Take State 400 south from Buffalo for fifteen miles; better yet, take Alternate Route US 20 from the east.

The first time my family visited East Aurora, we were in search of the Millard Fillmore house. We walked down the Main Street of fresh-scrubbed brick storefronts and stepped into an antique emporium. We asked the shopkeeper where President Fillmore's house might be. He squinted, thought a bit, and shrugged.

"Dunno," he said. "Never heard of it. But Harry Hamlin's people lived on ——— Street."

Sic transit gloria mundi, and all hail the virile star of television's "L.A. Law."

East Aurora is a gorgeous village about fifteen miles south of Buffalo. It's become pricier over the last several years, and a number of football's Buffalo Bills have moved into town. (Whatever you do, don't mention the Super Bowl in East Aurora.) But the village retains the maple leafy, black shutters, and white clapboard charm of a Ray Bradbury Illinois story.

The village is nestled in the southwestern corner of Erie

County. "Take the train for East Aurory, Where we work for Art and Glory," rhymed Elbert Hubbard, but you can get there by following Alternate Route US 20 from the east or State 400 south from Buffalo. Lucky you if you take US 20: this is hilly land, green and forested, full of dips and folds and undulations. Dairy farms line the road, and the grazing kine are a picture of stupid contentment.

One of the greatest of all American eccentrics, Elbert Hubbard, called East Aurora home, and the site of his colony of craftsmen at the corner of Main and Grove streets is now a National Historic Landmark District. The fourteen-building campus houses antique shops and boutiques and artisans and potters working more or less in the Roycroft tradition sired by Mr. Hubbard.

How does one begin to describe Elbert Hubbard?

In appearance, according to one biographer, he wore "a large Buster Brown cravat, baggy corduroys, flannel shirt, farmer's brogans, and western Stetson. His hair was naturally curly, and he let it grow to his shoulders, giving a pageboy effect."

He was a salesman extraordinaire with the Larkin Soap Company in Buffalo and a genius at advertising who nursed literary ambitions like a swollen thumb. When his submissions to the popular magazines of the day came back attached to rejection slips, the thirty-nine-year-old Hubbard did what any frustrated wealthy writer would do: start his own magazine. He named it *The Philistine*, in defiance of the literary establishment that had rebuffed him, and he appointed himself "General Inspector of the Universe."

The Philistine was a thirty-two-page hodgepodge of epigrams, clever ads, sermonettes by the agnostic Hubbard (who jocularly referred to himself as "The Pastor" and "Fra Elbertus"), contributions by a diverse stable of Hubbardites including young Stephen Crane, jokes that would make a *Reader's Digest* humor editor wince, and megalomaniacal self-promotion that would shame Norman Mailer. His 1899 hortatory tale, "A Message to Garcia," a tribute to good old American initiative and the can-do spirit, was reprinted an astonishing forty million times. His readers included

Secretary of State John Hay, British Prime Minister William Glad-
stone, and temperance leader Frances Willard (a native of the tidy
village of Churchville, fifty miles to the west).

But *The Philistine* was just one of Elbert's many ventures.
He founded a colony of craftsmen, the Roycrofters, named after
seventeenth-century English bookbinders, and on this "culture
farm" he grew printers, painters, sculptors, and book-and-furni-
turemakers. He marched in the vanguard—on the far left flank,
admittedly—of the American Arts and Crafts movement that
flourished in the first two decades of our century; his guild, unlike
other such communities, thrived.

At their peak, the Roycrofters numbered over one thousand,
and in keeping with Hubbard's libertarian philosophy each worker
decided what his or her own job would be. So you wanna be a bookbinder? Okay, you're a bookbinder. Learn the trade and go to it.
The Hubbardites were the hippie individualists of their day.

Many regarded Elbert Hubbard as a mountebank, a fraud, a
sham prophet born too late for the Burned-Over nonsense. He was
not scrupulous as regards the facts in some of his writings, and the
quality of Roycroft bookmaking is, to put it mildly, a matter of some
dispute among bibliophiles. While married to his first wife, he conducted a flagrant affair with a freethinking woman just outside of
town, and scandalized tongues wagged.

Elbert, a committed pacifist, went down on the *Lusitania*, en
route to preach the gospel of peace in war-ravaged Europe. The
Roycrofters soldiered on into the 1930s before they, too, abandoned ship. As Hubbard's son explained, "Up against ruthless
competition in a machine age, we had either to give up our business
or the ideals of artistic handcraftsmanship. . . . We did not desert
our ideals."

One block south and one block east of the Main Street campus is the Elbert Hubbard Library Museum at 363 Oakwood
Avenue. This green bungalow belonged to Gladys and George
ScheideMantel; she was the daughter of the Roycroft Inn's cook,
he was an accomplished leatherworker. Their home, built by Roycrofters, is now a museum administered by the energetic Aurora

Historical Society. It's open Wednesday, Saturday, and Sunday afternoons from June until mid-October.

Our guides, Beckey Moffet and Bruce Bland, pointed out pottery, paintings, armchairs, stained glass, vases, and furnishings made by Roycrofters. The heavy furniture is too darkly severe for most tastes, but then I'm a lotus-eating sybarite who dreams of Barcaloungers. The museum contains twelve oils by Alexis Jean Fournier, the noted turn-of-the-century Roycroft painter, and several recent works by local artist Rixford Jennings.

If you can, time your visit to coincide with either the Roycroft Summer or Winter Festival of Arts, held over two antipodal weekends. The festivals, sponsored by Roycrofters-at-Large, feature performances, artwork, crafts, and my favorite combination, food and fellowship. Contemporary Roycrofters sell their wares, and Elbert himself is there in spirit. "Let's see! Let's see!" he used to say. "What is it they pursue in Boston? Culture! That's it! In East Aurora we don't have to pursue Culture. She feels at home and abides with us!"

Talk is that the old Roycroft Inn may reopen. Restoration is proceeding apace, but hassles with government bureaucrats have slowed things a bit. When completed, the inn and an accompanying restaurant will be must-sees. (The National Trust for Historic Preservation placed the inn on its Top Ten Endangered Sites list a few years back.)

Carl Sandburg, the "People, Yes!" poet, made a pilgrimage to the village at the age of twenty-four and was star struck. "I went away from that place with a kind of lump in my throat and a gladness in my heart . . . When future generations weigh in the balance the life of Elbert Hubbard," he predicted, "they will pronounce him one of the greatest men the world ever saw."

Well, not quite, Carl.

Elbert Hubbard used to lecture in the castellated stone meeting hall on the corner of Main and South Grove that now houses the Aurora Historical Museum. Constructed in 1899, it contains Indian tools, arrowheads, and the like. A series of murals by Rixford Jennings depicts the history of the town. The tour is self-guided and takes a matter of minutes. When you're done, walk through the building, which contains a variety of local government offices, and admire the Roycroft-made doors and moldings.

Rix Jennings gets around: he also did the stained-glass windows at the St. Matthias Episcopal Church, a few blocks west on Main Street. Almost catercornered to St. Matthias, the Baker Memorial United Methodist Church has seventeen opalescent glass windows, several of which were designed by Louis Comfort Tiffany.

Inspect the two bronzed sculptures in front of the East Aurora Main Street School. One, sculpted by Irish Roycrofter Jerome Connor in 1930, is of Fra Elbertus himself, and the other is a replica of Paul Bartlett's figure of Michelangelo. No one ever accused Elbert and his Roycrofters of modesty.

Now take the short walk down Shearer Avenue to number 24, the Millard and Abigail Fillmore House.

Millard moved to East Aurora from Central New York with his parents, farming folk, in 1822. He built this home with his own hands for his bride Abigail in 1826. He was a young lawyer handling the petty trade of a small village, and he climbed the social ladder with his native intelligence (he had little formal schooling) and easy charm. He became active in the brief brilliant comet know as the Anti-Masonic party, which for a lustrum or so was the dominant political party in the Burned-Over District.

(The party grew out of a suspicion that the Masonic Order, which we now think of as a harmless fraternal lodge, was a secret society intent on subverting the republic. When an itinerant alcoholic Batavian named William Morgan prepared a book revealing the theretofore hidden secrets of Masonry—codes, oaths, and the like—he was jailed on a possibly trumped-up charge of theft, then spirited from the jail in Canandaguia and . . . well, no one quite knows. The commonest explanation of Morgan's disappearance is that he was drowned in the Niagara River. Some Masons deny it to this day; they claim Morgan lived out a long and bibulous life in Canada. Whatever the truth, Morgan's dramatic exit from the stage lit the brushfire that became the Anti-Masonic Party, forerunner of the Whigs. A cenotaph was erected to Morgan's memory in 1880 in the Batavia Cemetery on Harvester Avenue.)

Now back to Millard. Fillmore was elected to the New York State Assembly in 1828 as an Anti-Mason. Two years later he and his wife Abigail moved to Buffalo. From there it was Congress, and after a checkered career full of intrigues involving the colorful New York Whig bosses William Seward and Thurlow Weed, Fillmore won the party's vice presidential nomination in 1848 on a ticket headed by General Zachary Taylor.

Millard Fillmore, future President of the United States,
built this house by hand in 1826

Old Rough-and-Ready defeated the bland Democratic candidate, Lewis Cass, and in 1850, beset by too much sun and too many iced cherries at an Independence Day celebration, the president departed this vale of tears. Millard Fillmore became President of the United States. (You may recall a couple of years ago, when President Taylor's corpse was exhumed to determine if he'd been poisoned. Fillmore was exonerated, to East Aurora's relief.)

Millard Fillmore served only two years as president; he is best remembered for signing the Fugitive Slave Act and for his efforts to conciliate the South. In 1856 he accepted the presidential nomination of the American party, somewhat unfairly dubbed the "Know-Nothings." The party included nativists who suspected Catholics of disloyalty, but Fillmore conducted an honorable campaign, free of bigotry, and he won 28 percent of the popular vote nationwide. His political career over, Fillmore settled into his role as First Citizen of Buffalo, becoming the first president of that booming port city's historical society.

Astonishingly, Millard Fillmore's Buffalo home was destroyed by the wrecker's ball in 1923 to make way for a hotel. A hospital and school and suchlike are named for him in Buffalo—"This self-important Buffalo," an "ant-hill so absurd," as Vachel Lindsay angrily versified—but in East Aurora, however fleeting Fillmore's stay was, he is best honored.

The Fillmore home in East Aurora, a small frame structure in the Greek Revival style, used to stand on Main Street where now there is a theater. Mrs. Margaret Price, wife of the Fisher-Price toy magnate, bought and moved it to its present location in 1930; she fancied herself an artist and used it as a studio. In 1975 the Aurora Historical Society purchased the building and went about restoring it.

The Fillmore House is filled with furniture and dolls, shotguns and other artifacts of the time, not all of them traceable to Millard. The docents are knowledgeable Fillmore buffs. My favorite room, the parlor, dark and funereal on even the sunniest days due to the heavy curtains, features a striking portrait of the president painted in 1871 by Augustus Rockwell. Queen Victoria called Fillmore the handsomest man she had ever seen; perhaps he was born a century too soon. A rose and herb garden planted and tended by the East Aurora Garden Club is as impressive, if not more, as the modest home.

East Aurora holds a birthday party for Millard Fillmore every January 7 at the venerable (circa 1824) Globe Hotel and Restaurant, a.k.a., Tony Rome's, at 711 Main Street. (Yes, Millard himself stabbed a fork on the premises.) Guests sup on stew and corn bread and apple cobbler while the president (or a close facsimile) is serenaded with "The Millard Fillmore Birthday Song" and given a "This is Your Life" tour by proud if somewhat irreverent Aurorans. There's also a Christmas sale at the house on the first Saturday in December, featuring baked goods and handmade toys and handicrafts. For the rest of winter, though, the museum is closed. It reopens with the peonies in June and closes about the time the leaves drop from the trees in mid-fall. A very modest admission fee is charged.

Independence Day Weekend in East Aurora is given to the usual chivaree. The atmosphere is festively middle American, with a parade, a barbeque, a pig roast, a laser light show, horseshoes, a clogging demonstration, and the consumption of prodigious quantities of hot dogs and pop and beer. (Yes, "pop." The quickest way to spot an outsider in upstate New York is to hear her call a carbonated beverage "soda.")

The revelries run down Main Street out to Hamlin Park—and you already know whose family that's named for, don't you? The Hamlins were trotting-horse people, as were (and are) the Knoxes, endowers of the Albright-Knox Art Gallery, in Buffalo, and the East Aurora-based owners of the perenially mediocre Buffalo Sabres of the National Hockey League. Even the Fra himself said, "No man can have melancholia who loves a horse and is understood by one."

Throughout the summer Hamlin Park hosts a series of concerts under the stars. Bring a lawn chair or blanket and watch the August moon come up while the sweet notes of a barbershop quartet or jazz band fill the air. Hamlin Park is on Grove Street, two blocks from the Roycroft campus.

As you walk down Main Street, look for the red and white awning and step in to Vidler's five-and-ten. It's packed with crafts, Fisher-Price toys, penny (well, quarter) candies, and a 1918 machine that guesses your weight and predicts your fortune as you gaze into a full-length mirror. A nickel or dime won't buy much at Vidler's—"MasterCard and VISA accepted," declares a sign I don't recall seeing in Batavia's old five-and-ten shops—but it's a nice homey place nevertheless.

East Aurora, at least its commercial aspect, still seems devoted to Art and Glory. Antique shops and art galleries and impressive churches line Main Street, and a browser—or votary—can make a pleasing day of it.

ToyFest is later in August, usually on the last weekend. Besides Hubbard and Hamlin and Fillmore, East Aurora is home to the Fisher-Price toy company, whose wages have paid for many of the attractive two-story homes that line the side streets of the town. Fisher-Price was established in 1930 and today employs almost one thousand people at its local plant.

ToyFest calls itself "a celebration of childhood," and it provides enough juvenile fun and amusement to keep Michael Jackson and Steven Spielberg happy. A parade, an antique toy show, giant slides, a fun house, and various frolicsome events fill Hamlin Park and other sites. Artisans and artists sell their creations in the parking lot on the Roycroft campus. In a stroke of offbeat promotion Elbert Hubbard would've loved, hundreds of kids design crates and packages for raw eggs, which are then dropped 200 feet by a cherry picker. The winners retrieve their eggs—intact. Most of the ovoids go the Humpty-Dumpty route, so it's a lot of messy fun.

ToyTown Museum at 650 Main Street, East Aurora's newest attraction, really hums during ToyFest. It includes all manner of playthings, from colonial-era dolls to space-age gadgetry, and it is expanding every year.

If you're in town on any of eight fall Sundays (or Mondays), the Buffalo Bills will be playing just six miles west down State Alt 20 in Orchard Park. When the team is doing well, tickets are rare as scrawny fullbacks, but if, as local pessimists suspect, the Bills

48

are due for a drought after several outstanding seasons, ducats can be had.

East Aurora is a delightful town: prosperous, tidy, historically minded and, well, a wee bit outré. For years, purveyors of conventional wisdom have called Hubbard a charlatan and Fillmore a craven pro-Southern doughface. I think rather more highly of both men, but no matter: whatever their quirks or crotchets, their memories fare well in this lively town. Elbert Hubbard used to say, "Every knock is a boost," and his East Aurory boosters prove him right.

Aurora Historical Museum, 716-652-3280
East Aurora Chamber of Commerce, 716-652-8444
Elbert Hubbard Museum, 716-652-4735
Millard Fillmore House, 716-652-3280
ToyTown Museum, 716-655-3888
Vidler's Five-and-Ten, 716-652-0481

6

Hyde Park

From Albany, take US 9 south. Or take the thruway south to Exit 18 (New Paltz), then take State 299 east, US 9W south, cross the Mid-Hudson Bridge, and go north on US 9. From New York City, take the Taconic State Parkway north, exit at State 55 west, and take US 9 north.

Hyde Park is a small, somewhat shaggy Hudson Valley town which could be called unpretentious were it not the sanctuary of Vanderbilts and Roosevelts, fascinating families that have been called many things but never modest.

This is Dutch country; the town was called Stoutenberg from 1742 until Anglophiles changed the name in 1812. (The Stoutenberg homestead, a stone farmhouse, circa 1750, is on State 9G just two miles up the road from Val-Kill, about which more later.) The county name, Dutchess, is derived from Maria Beatrice D'Este, the Dutchess of York who later became Queen Mary. Fittingly, the town was once the caviar-producing capital of the New World, until the sturgeon disappeared from the Hudson River seventy-five years ago.

No, the eggs were not hoarded by Commodore Vanderbilt, though enemies in robber baron–land wouldn't have been surprised. Cornelius Vanderbilt, "the Commodore," was a colorful capitalist buccaneer who made his first fortune in the steamship trade and then really hit the jackpot when he took over the New York Central Railroad, which was the engine that made the Vanderbilts the richest American family of the 1870s. (The New York Central, if I may be forgiven a personal note, was built up by a rogue from my hometown of Batavia, Dean Richmond.)

Cornelius Vanderbilt bought politicians as other men purchase Big Macs, and even his official biographer admitted that the Commodore was "puffed with divine greed." He kept his cigars in a pocket rather than a cigar case so that when he removed one "my friends don't know whether there are any left," and therefore they wouldn't dun him for smokes.

But he was a character, and if we must have plutocrats better a Commodore Vanderbilt than some faceless front man for a multinational conglomerate. Living by the maxim, never tell nobody what yer goin' to do till you do it, the Commodore had a flair for the grand gesture. At the age of sixty-seven, he asked President Lincoln for permission to captain the steamship *Vanderbilt* into battle against the Confederacy's storied ironclad *Merrimac*. He had a dozen children; William Henry, the son he belittled as "beetlehead" and "good for nothing," was bequeathed the bulk of the Commodore's $100 million estate upon his death in 1877.

Beetlehead turned out to have a noggin for business; he doubled the size of the Vanderbilt fortune. (He also uttered the immortal line, "The public be damned!" though William Henry's defenders insist that the remark was uttered in defense of his stockholders.)

William Henry had eight children. Most were fools and wastrels who scattered the fortune to the winds, but a middle son, Frederick—a shy, retiring, childless man—alchemized his $10 million inheritance into $70 million by his death in 1938. Among Frederick's several homes his favorite was the Beaux-Arts limestone mansion at Hyde Park, designed by Stanford White and his partners in 1895.

The estate, treed and resplendent in autumn, is on the east bank of the Hudson River. The visitor's center, formerly the guest

The Vanderbilt mansion overlooking the Hudson

house where bachelors bunked for the night, is larger than most upper-middle class residences. Today it contains exhibits chronicling the Vanderbilt empire as well as a neat gift shop.

Walk a winding path for a hundred or so yards and there it is, the stern beige temple that inspires a thousand "wow's" a day and sets one to thinking about the way in which descendants of the nouveau *really* riche run from the men who amassed the loot.

This fifty-room home built by America's most hypertrophied fortune is not really American at all. The third generation of Vanderbilts, far enough removed from the Commodore to lament his vulgarity while spending his money, fancied themselves analogues of the European nobility, so French and Italian accents in this home are far louder than the American vernacular, which could be heard only in the voices of the sixty or so local families that tended the grounds during the Vanderbilts' lengthy absences. (The family spent summers in Newport, Rhode Island, and winters in New York City.) The spirit of Louis Quinze dominates the Gold reception room, designed by Georges Glaenzer, and the first floor rooms of Stanford White are peppered with items the architect found in Paris, London, Florence, Rome, and Venice.

You wouldn't call Frederick's taste understated. Tapestries bedeck the walls, as paintings by Hudson Valley artists do not. Be sure to see Mrs. Vanderbilt's bedroom; a railing surrounds the bed, in the fashion of French queens, to keep the hoi polloi—and perhaps her husband—at bay. A grand old woman played the piano as we surveyed the deep and sumptuous living room. Railroads and steamships are quite foreign to this palace.

The Vanderbilt Mansion, administered by the National Park Service, is open from 9:00 A.M. to 5:00 P.M. every day but holidays and winter weekends. The admission is modest, unlike the home, and you'll want to amble about the grounds, taking special notice of the restored Italian gardens and the view of the Hudson. The tour is self-guided, but rangers are stationed throughout the home; we found Wayne Gilchrest particularly helpful. The second floor of the visitor's center houses the Hyde Park Historical Society Museum.

Hyde Park was home to plutes and pols, as an alliterative plebe might say. Not even two miles up US 9 the Roosevelts, Dutch-English patroons, lived in the home they called Springwood. James Roosevelt, father of the future president, bought Springwood in the 1860s, and over the next half century it underwent more alterations and renovations than an aging actress' face. His only child, Franklin, a dabbler in architecture, supervised its final makeover (in the neo-Georgian style) in 1915.

Franklin Delano Roosevelt was born to James and Sara at Springwood on January 30, 1882. Educated away—he certainly did not attend Hyde Park public schools, but he later helped force their consolidation—he returned in 1905 with his bride Eleanor, his fifth cousin once removed. Springwood was to be his primary non-Washington residence for the remainder of his life.

The Squire of Hyde Park, who as a lad was mocked as a mama's boy, excelled in the hurly-burly of politics, winning the governorship of New York in 1928 and the presidency in 1932, an office from which only death could dislodge him.

The home is done up in Hudson Valley Victorian: the woods are dark, the furnishings bespeak a family that is prosperous but sensible. Naval prints—dozens and dozens of them—line the walls, along with the usual ancestral portraits (including a Gilbert Stuart portrait of Isaac Roosevelt, Franklin's great-great-grandfather.) Prince Pierre Troubetzkey's rendering of Sara Roosevelt is stunning, in early adulthood, Franklin looked exactly like his mother! Now I understand why mischievous Alice Roosevelt called her cousin "Nancy."

Several pieces in the Main Hall, notably the eighteenth-century grandfather clock, were purchased by James in the Netherlands, befitting our last Dutch president. Be sure to see Fala's leash and blanket in the president's bedroom on the second floor; one guesses that this Scottie's pampered existence made Millie Bush's and Checkers Nixon's seem like dog's lives.

The FDR library and museum, also on the premises, is constructed of local fieldstone. Dedicated in 1941, it was the first of the bibliothecal cathedrals presidents have built to themselves.

Exhibits chronicling the life and presidency of Franklin (and the considerable contributions of Eleanor) highlight the library and museum. FDR's collection of miniature ships is on display; he was a maritime buff, after all, an assistant secretary of the navy under President Wilson, and one wonders how he felt to see his pleasant daydreams about warfare on the high seas concretize—in horrifying reality—during the Second World War.

The president's 1936 Ford Phaeton, specially equipped so he could drive, is a favorite of visitors. So is his bassinet. In his study, one can even hear his taped speeches in that reassuring patrician tone.

One ticket admits the visitor to the home and the library and museum, which are open every day but Christmas, Thanksgiving, and New Year's Day. Tours are self-guided, and on busy days the place is packed. Across the street, for those who like their juxtapositions sharp, is the Hyde Park Drive-In Theater.

"She found little comfort in visiting" Hyde Park, Eleanor's son Elliott wrote in *The Hyde Park Murder* (1985), one of a string of mysteries he has written with his mother as the sleuthing heroine. "The mansion was not her home but the home and domain of her redoubtable mother-in-law, Sara Delano Roosevelt, who would find plenty of occasions . . . to remind her daughter-in-law of the shortcomings she found in her."

Eleanor quite understandably needed a respite from Sara's caviling, and she found it at Val-Kill, east of Springwood on State 9G. Val-Kill (named for a nearby stream) consisted of two cottages: a modest Dutch Colonial made of fieldstone, which was home to Eleanor's friends Nancy Cook and Marion Dickerman, and a larger building that served first as the site of Val-Kill Industries and later as Eleanor's private residence.

Val-Kill Industries was a noble failed experiment. Eleanor and her friends employed local people to make reproduction furniture and other products in an Early American style. She fancied herself a potential "female Henry Ford," and she hoped the factory would provide employment for farm laborers in winter.

Val-Kill, also known as the Eleanor Roosevelt National Historic

Site, is open on spring weekends and every day from May until October. Admission is free. A film biography of Eleanor is shown to visitors, who may wander through both cottages and among the flower gardens and bosky trails.

Eleanor was a do-gooder to the *nth* degree, but the visitor is likely to come away feeling kinder toward her than her husband. The novelist Henry W. Clune, my 103-year-old friend, was the staunchest of anti-New Deal Republicans, yet he retains a soft spot in his heart for Mrs. Roosevelt, whom he knew and admired. Even those who deplore Franklin's legacy may not be immune to the sincere noblesse oblige of the solicitous matron of Val-Kill.

The president's church, St. James Episcopal, is across the road from the Vanderbilt Mansion. Designed by an amateur architect, Augustus Thomas Coleman, and built in 1844 as an English Tudor with castellated refinements, St. James was gutted by fire in 1984. Drop in on Sunday morning at 8:00 or 10:00 A.M. for services and to peek at its reconstruction.

It's easy to forget in Hyde Park that history is not made solely by great men. The village itself bears the Rooseveltian stamp. The post office at the corner of East Market Street and US 9 was a WPA project, built of fieldstone in 1940, when the president was reinvolving himself in Hyde Park affairs in anticipation of his forever-deferred retirement. He and Postmaster James Farley attended its dedication, a gala event. As you'd expect, the Hyde Park Post Office is no Podunk affair. The walls inside feature murals by Hudson River Valley painter Olin Dows, a friend of the president. Why drop your postcards in a street-corner box when you can take in an art show?

The Hyde Park Free Library across the street at 2 Main Street was donated in 1927 by Franklin's mother Sara to memorialize her late husband James Roosevelt. Sara was an imperious woman—as poor Eleanor knew too well—and because she had endowed the library she saw no reason why she should return overdue books she liked.

For a reminder of the *other* Hyde Park, the one-room Little Red Schoolhouse still stands upon the grounds of the North Park

Elementary School on State 9G. Call the school principal or the Hyde Park Historical Society to arrange a look. And realize that the Squire of Hyde Park was not universally loved by his neighbors: FDR ran for office nine times, and carried his hometown but thrice.

The region is rich in antiques, though as a general rule the closer one gets to New York City the higher the price tag. Still, bargains can be had, especially by those with a keen eye, a taste for down-at-the-heels junk shops, and the haggling acumen of the Dutchmen who bought Manhattan Island.

In the midst of such opulent wealth and overweening power, it's no surprise to find the CIA. The Hyde Park institution of that acronym is entirely benign—indeed, it is an epicure's delight. The Culinary Institute of America, founded in 1946, is an internationally known school consecrated to the training of chefs and other culinary professionals.

Founded in 1946, the CIA moved to its current site, a former Jesuit seminary, in 1972. (The Catholic philosopher Pierre Teilhard de Chardin is buried on the grounds.) Tours are only available for groups of twenty or more, but the institute operates four restaurants that are open to the public every day but Sunday. The CIA is just three miles south of the village of Hyde Park on US 9. Spies, moles, and even English art students with Communist sympathies are welcome.

The Waugh family of artists are featured in the Edward A. Ulrich Museum, one mile north of the Vanderbilt Mansion on US 9. Housed in an old barn, the collection is open for inspection by those who call ahead.

Five miles north of Hyde Park on US 9 is the Beaux-Arts mansion of financier Ogden Mills. Designed by Stanford White in 1895, this is every bit as massive as the Vanderbilt mansion: there are sixty-five rooms and fourteen bathrooms. The interior design is predominately seventeenth and eighteenth century French. The Mills family gave the property to New York State in 1938; it is open from May until October on Wednesday through Sunday.

It's tough for a visitor to really comprehend Hyde Park, a town of strip malls and mansions, drive-ins and presidents. So just enjoy. Here are two separate worlds, and never the twain shall meet, even on US 9.

Culinary Institute of America, 914-471-6608
Dutchess County Tourism Promotion Agency, 914-229-0033
Edward A. Ulrich Museum, 914-229-7107
Eleanor Roosevelt National Historic Site (Val-Kill), 914-229-9115
Franklin D. Roosevelt Library and Museum, 914-229-8114
Home of Franklin D. Roosevelt National Historic Site, 914-229-9115
Hyde Park Free Library, 914-229-7791
Hyde Park Historical Society, 914-229-2310
Mills Mansion State Historic Site, 914-889-4100
North Park Elementary School, 914-229-9101
Vanderbilt Mansion National Historic Site, 914-229-9115

7

Hammondsport

On State 54A, five miles north of the Bath Exit on Interstate 17 and forty miles northwest of Elmira.

Hammondsport, located on the southern tip of Keuka Lake, is a bit ethereal, perhaps even flighty, which makes sense, because its reputation is based on airplanes and wine, and between the two visitors' feet hardly touch the ground.

The Keuka—"Crooked Lake" the settlers called it—is shaped like a Y, or a chicken bone not yet pulled apart. The beautiful towns of Hammondsport and Penn Yan sit at its antipodes. Both are worth visits, but the former is so distinguished it has two nicknames— "the cradle of aviation" and "the grape bowl."

You've heard of the Wright brothers but perhaps not of Glenn Hammond Curtiss, the aeronautical pioneer who piloted the "June Bug" 5,090 feet on Independence Day, 1908, on aviation's first pre-announced flight. He made the short but giant jaunt at Stony Brook Farm just outside his hometown of Hammondsport. The June Bug achieved the sublunary height of twenty feet; hundreds of onlookers marveled; many ran alongside the craft, cheering as it remained aloft. Curtiss won fame and a silver trophy worth $2,500 from *Scientific American* for his "practical aerodrome driven by its own motive power and carrying a man."

Curtiss was a whiz kid, a bicycle-race champ back when the sport was a national craze. He set up his own shop, where he made bicycles, then motorcycles, then balloons, and finally the flying machines that turned Hammondsport into a beehive of aviation activity. Inventors and geniuses and oddballs of all sorts visited Hammondsport, including Alexander Graham Bell, a partner of Glenn's in the Aerial Experiment Association of 1907. "The sky was full of flying machines," remembered one local writer.

The aviator himself was slight and diffident, with a balding dome that hardly suggested daredeviltry. His "Curtiss barnstormers" thrilled earthbound sky gazers, and the list of his accomplishments is weighted with firsts: he started the first flying school, won the first International Speed Trophy, made the first flight over ocean water and the first long-distance trip (from Albany to New York City).

The Curtiss factory in Hammondsport profited greatly from the First World War: Britain alone placed an order totaling $14 million. In time, demand for Curtiss' product swelled so that he shifted his base of operations to Buffalo, and you can imagine the hard feelings that engendered. Nevertheless, when Glenn H. Curtiss died in 1930, he was buried at Pleasant Valley Cemetery on State 54.

The Glenn H. Curtiss Museum is at 8419 State 54, one mile north of the cemetery. Housed in a 56,000 square foot whilom wine warehouse, the museum is dedicated to Curtiss' kinetic passions: bicycles, motorcycles, and above all airplanes and the engines that make them run.

A highlight is the replica of the June Bug built in 1976 by volunteers from Hammondsport's Mercury Aircraft. But the Curtiss cupola is the museum's real anchor. The family homestead on Castle Hill burned in 1969 and was razed three years later; only this cupola, which Curtiss called his "thinkorium," was salvaged.

He must have spent hours cogitating in his thinkorium over those dastardly Wright brothers. The Wrights endlessly pestered Curtiss with patent infringement suits, some of which were successful, and even today the boys from Kitty Hawk are about as popular in Hammondsport as a Miami Dolphins fan in Buffalo. "The

Wrights were interested in themselves," argues museum curator Lindsley A. Dunn. "They cared about money and were obsessed with suing everyone. Glenn Curtiss was interested in promoting aviation." A T-shirt on sale in the Curtiss gift shop asks "Wilbur and Orville Who?"

The Curtiss Museum is open every day of the year except holidays. (Hours are somewhat truncated when the hoarfrost gives way to snow.) The admission is $4 for adults, less for children and the elderly. This museum is poised for takeoff, no pun intended, volunteers are plentiful, and coffers are overflowing. The ambitious master plan calls for this vast museum to tell the story of one man with a dream and the community that nourished him.

The southern Finger Lakes region, brilliantly verdant with grapevines in summertime, has nourished the dreams of countless imbibers as well. Nine wineries dot the local countryside; six welcome visitors.

America's oldest continuing maker of wines is the Pleasant Valley Wine Company, which was purchased by the Taylor Wine Company in 1961 and is now under absentee ownership. Pleasant Valley was founded by a baker's dozen of would-be vintners in 1860; the driving force was a French grape-grower named Charles D. Champlin, and if the name sounds familiar it's because his great-grandson Charles Champlin has for years been the movie critic of the Los Angeles Times. Young Charles grew up in Hammondsport in the 1930s and 1940s and wrote a charming book of reminiscences, *Back There Where the Past Was*, which is required reading for any visitor. (His boyhood home at 51 Lake Street still stands.)

"Hammondsport was rural, I suppose," writes Champlin, "but the wine and the flying gave it, in this century certainly, a cosmopolitan flavor that not many outlying towns its size had."

You can see what has become of the Champlin family business at the Taylor-Great Western-Gold Seal Winery on County 88, open six days a week throughout the year (and also on Sundays in summer).

Keeping track of who owns what in wine country is confounding. Take Taylor.

Walter Taylor founded the Taylor Wine Company in 1880. It endures, but its fiercest and most irrepressible critic is one Walter Taylor, a lineal descendant. The Taylor surname was the subject of one of the strangest court battles in the annals of American business.

The contemporary Walter Taylor is president of the small, doughty, and savory Bully Hill Winery and he is one of American industry's great eccentrics. Walter was booted out of the winery that bore his name in 1970 when he made a blistering public attack on what he claimed were its dubious practices. So Walter and his father began their own winery up on Bully Hill. Coca-Cola, which in 1977 bought out Taylor Wine, sued to keep Walter from using the family name on the wine labels of his new company. The case wended its way through the courts and Walter became a cause célebrè. He lost, but he won: a showman who makes Barnum look like a shrinking violet, Walter ostentatiously blotted out the Taylor name on his Bully Hill labels, brochures, and price lists in a manner that drew even more attention to him.

"They have my name and heritage," he declared, "but they didn't get my goat"; nor did they rob him of his outlandishness. An artsy military school graduate whose antics are the stuff of legend in Hammondsport, Taylor draws all his own labels; they are dreamy and vatic and quasireligious, with goats and angels and remembrances of his daughter, who died several years ago in an accident. Walter himself was badly injured in a recent car crash, but Bully Hill's labels remain classics of Burned-Over artwork.

This bohemian cadet's peculiar visions of the peaceable kingdom are on display at the Greyton Hoyt Taylor Wine Museum on Bully Hill Road, the only wine museum in America, or so it boasts. It also contains a large collection of the tools of the vintner's art, as well as the vitreous vessels that convey the nectar from barrel to lip. White House Glassware is a favorite exhibit: the Lincoln family's goblets are here, as are the champagne glasses sipped — and slurped — from by President Nixon and Chinese Premier Chou En-Lai. You're welcome to visit every day from April 15 until November.

Hammondsport

The Heron Hill Winery, three miles north of Hammondsport on County 76, offers a commanding view of the lake and the vineyards. Tours are given from May through November and are by appointment only.

Curtiss, Champlin, Taylor, and the others were a godsend, because the Erie Railroad had ignored Hammondsport and the Crooked Lake Canal, which connected Keuka and Seneca Lakes, hadn't been the boon its boosters had hoped for. Moreover, a series of fires destroyed much of Hammondsport's nineteenth-century lakeside downtown; chastened, merchants rebuilt on higher ground.

A handsome village square is the heart of Hammondsport. An ornate bandstand, built in 1892 for less than $400, makes for a bully pulpit. (Craftsman Leonard Fiorito constructed a wonderful miniature replica of the bandstand at a scale of one foot to one inch. See it at the Curtiss Museum.)

Every Fourth of July the flags of the thirteen colonies are hoisted over the green to the discharge of rifles as an orator reads the Declaration of Independence. A week or two later the Keuka Lake Art Association Show fills the square, then in August an annual craft show takes the baton. The Hammondsport Antique Show and Sale, sponsored by the Wine Country Tourism Association, is held in June at the Main Street School.

Bed and breakfasts dot the grapey vales of the Keuka bioregion. Edwin N. Harris, a fine local writer and memorialist, spent his honeymoon half a century ago at a Hammondsport establishment, the Park Inn on the Village Square, where lodging is spacious and the drink flows, especially when Ed is near the bar. Co-owner John Jensen showed us the restaurant and the four nicely appointed double rooms in this circa-1861 hostelry; a gift shop is on the premises, and the adjacent Crooked Lake Ice Cream Company can satisfy your craving for frozen delectations.

Up Sheather Street, past the faded but still readable lettering above the long-gone Smellie's Drugs (was ever an apothecary so unfortunately named?), is the Opera House, a 1902 Romanesque edifice. No, Caruso never sang there, but magicians and hypnotists dazzled their audiences until the fire marshals closed it down. The opera house is now occupied by gift and antique shops.

The slate sidewalks of Lake Street lead right down to their crooked inspiration. The green "ink bottle house" at 17 Sheather is striking; it's now the J. S. Hubbs Bed and Breakfast. One block parallel, at 7 William Street, is town eponym Lazarus Hammond's home, which dates from 1810 and, at this writing, looks it.

The lake has always attracted summer people, though the social division between estivating outlanders and year-rounders is said to be narrow enough. A cool, refreshing dip in the lake is a great leveler; among the public swimming swatches is Champlin Beach. (No, the water is not transmuted to wine.) Local natatorialists, however, bad-mouth Champlin Beach—"too shallow" and "kinda polluted" we were told—and instead recommend the public beach at the end of Sheather Street.

While splashing around you'll catch sight of the 170-ton *Keuka Maid*, which carries as many as 400 passengers on its lunch, dinner, and Sunday-brunch cruises up and down the crooked lake from May through October. The boat is a popular spot for reunions and business meetings, so you're advised to call ahead for reservations. If you want victuals with your cruise, prices start at $17; a foodless excursion costs $10.

The hills surrounding Hammondsport offer stunning sights of Keuka; they're also populated by some fascinating characters. The Treichlers, Bill and Martha and their sons, Joe and John, live high above the lake on Mount Washington. Bill and Martha met at Black Mountain College in North Carolina, which was the proto-Beat generation capital of the 1940s, what with Charles Olson, Paul Goodman, John Cage, and other long-hairs roaming its grassy campus. After three decades of farming and teaching, the Treichlers bought nearly 100 acres of land in 1970, and from within their magnificently restored farmhouse they publish *The Crooked Lake Review*, a sprightly monthly devoted to local history and Finger Lakes culture. Get a copy before you visit: they're $2 each from 7988 Van Amburg Road, Hammondsport, NY 14840.

The less elevated Castle Hill at village's verge at the western terminus of Pulteney Street was the site of Glenn H. Curtiss' house and first factory. Today a school sits upon the ruins.

The Hammondsport Glen (wonder where Glenn Hammond Curtiss got his name?) is a ravine off Pulteney a block to the east. More than a century ago a local Barnum by the name of J.P. Barnes got the idea that the glen's stone walls and cataracts and defiles might turn him a profit. Watkins Glen, to the east, had become a favorite of sightseers, and if you've seen one glen you *haven't* seen them all. Alas, the Hammondsport Glen, after a brief spurt of popularity, sputtered as a commercial enterprise, and in later years Barnes was heard to denounce it as "the damned old gully."

The damned old gully is still there—and there's no Barnes to charge admission. Bring appropriate footgear.

On your way back to State 17, drive around the village of Bath, five miles south of town on State 54. More than thirty homes here are listed on the National Register of Historic Places. Bath was founded in 1793 by the foppish land agent Charles Williamson, a strange character described by Henry W. Clune as "perfumed and bewigged," flying about "on a blooded horse, in the prosecution of his spectacular enterprises." Bath he envisioned as the elegant capital of the western frontier, and though things didn't quite work out that way it's still an impressive town. One of America's foremost agricultural writers, John Rezelman, lives in Bath, and one can scarcely imagine a more fecund setting.

Farther up the road is Cohocton, home of Orson Fowler, the nineteenth-century genius behind the octagon house (see Chapter 3). One of the eight-sided wonders he inspired can be found in Hammondsport on County 88, a mile or so from the Taylor wineries. Its stone walls are eighteen inches thick.

Octagon homes are making a comeback of sorts: prefab models are selling here and there across America. It's hardly a craze yet, and the neighbors will scoff, as neighbors sometimes do, but then folks laughed at that Curtiss boy once, the retiring young fellow without much hair, always tinkering around his shop. A man with a dream and a thinkorium could change the world.

Glenn H. Curtiss Museum, 607-569-2160
Crooked Lake Review, 607-569-2382
Hammondsport Crafts Festival, 607-569-2242
Heron Hill Vineyards, 607-868-4241
J. S. Hubbs Bed and Breakfast, 607-569-2440
Keuka Art Association Show and Sale, 607-569-3564
Keuka Maid, 607-569-2628 or 569-3631
Park Inn Hotel, 607-569-9387
Taylor Winery Visitor Center, 607-569-6111
Wine Country Tourism Association, POB 452, Hammondsport, NY
    14840
Wine Museum of Greyton H. Taylor/Bully Hill, 607-868-4814/
    868-3490

8

Angelica

Take State 390 to Exit 36, then travel forty miles west on State 17. Or take State 19 and State 19A south from Warsaw for forty miles.

Allegany County is unlike any other in the state. Even denizens of my sleepy county of Genesee (population 60,000) deride Allegany as hick and its residents as hairy hillbillies who kill woodchucks with their bare hands and like to wash down a pot of possum stew with a jug of moonshine.

This is fantastically unfair, of course, but Allegany is a poor, hilly, sylvan shire, and many of its people live closer to the land than, say, your typical Rochesterian. Deer and wild turkeys (and, yes, Wild Turkey) are plentiful, and in season—or out, game wardens to the contrary—the woods ring with shotgun blasts as men and a surprising number of women kill the meat that will sustain them through the winter.

The state has not always treated Allegany with respect. In the late 1980s Albany determined to locate a low-level radioactive waste site here; the entire New York State establishment was in favor of placing the dump either in this hinterland or in Cortland County, neither of which has much money or clout or many votes. Then the citizens of Allegany did something that we're not used to anymore in this country founded by minutemen and rebels: they said no. Massive protests were held; state inspectors were kept off the threatened land—at gunpoint, in some instances. The people of Allegany County rose in concert and did what seemed impossible: they beat city hall—and the state hall.

The fight over the dump brought together the unlikeliest neighbors: churchgoing folk in nicely kept frame houses, long-hairs on Harleys, the solitary souls who live alone at the end of dirt roads, "outsider" professors who teach at Alfred University. This was one of the most inspiriting events in recent upstate history, a triumph of a county of Davids against the Albany Goliath, and the jests and potshots at Allegany, our hillbilly heaven, have lost their zip. (Rather in the way that Polish jokes disappeared when Solidarity sprang up.)

Angelica is the oldest town in Allegany County, and one of the strangest in all of New York. Imagine a proud and threadbare farm girl who traces her lineage back through the early American patriciate and the exiled French nobility. Typically, she will milk cows at dawn, take down a buck in the early morning, return to her stately columnar home, packed with heirlooms and dust, and stroll down to the village green at dusk, where she plays—with gamine skill—roque, a game that is a hybrid of croquet and billiards.

Angelica is not Hooterville, but it is not Saratoga either; you can't really call it quaint, nor is it dumpy. It manifests a kind of shabby gentility, though the lawns are mowed and the aristocrats have long since galloped into their purple sunsets.

The town was founded by Captain Philip Church, a nephew of Alexander Hamilton. Through his father's agency in 1800, Church obtained 100,000 acres of land in southwestern New York from the defaulting Robert Morris, the speculator and Declaration-signer who was then peering into the abyss of bankruptcy.

Captain Church, a dandyish man who took justified pride in his bloodline, named the village that he intended to be his regional capital Angelica, after his mother, the daughter of General Philip Schuyler.

Philip Church built a home for his new bride, Anna Matilda

Angelica

Stewart, a girl from the toniest Philadelphia society. Imagine her dismay when, on their first night in this forested remoteness, so far from all she had known, the couple had to sleep on straw mattresses and listen to wolves baying their minatory songs in the dark.

Their first rough dwelling, called the White House because it was the only painted structure in this part of the state, would not do at all. So in 1810 Philip built a manor of brick and stone overlooking the Genesee River, and there he and his bride lived out their years, the first couple of Allegany County. In best patroon tradition they named their lair—Belvidere—and they entertained Wadsworths and such. Among the family possessions were Hamilton's pistols, the ones that served him so poorly in his fatal duel with Aaron Burr. (John B. Church, Philip's father, also fought a duel with the roguish Burr; both missed, and they reconciled.)

Benjamin Latrobe may or may not have been the architect of Belvidere; the evidence weighs toward the negative. The mansion, two miles to the west of present-day Angelica, is visible from the road when the trees are denuded of leaves, but the only Churches around now are the lower-case kind. (The White House was blown down in a fierce storm in 1902.)

You may sense something French about the village, and I don't mean the fried potatoes at the Uptown Cafe. (A swanky name, by the way, for a fine little meat-and-potatoes diner at which ball-capped men with creased faces swap gossip and age-old jokes in warm fraternity.) A contingent of French Royalists settled in Angelica in 1806; Baron Hyde de Neuville, one of the exiles, later became France's Ambassador to the United States. Victor Marie du Pont de Nemours of the once and future rich du Ponts bought 500 acres from Church in 1805 and proceeded to go belly-up as a gentleman farmer. Poor Vic: he was just a century and a half too early for the better-farming-through-chemicals craze.

Arch Merrill, the Rochester newspaperman, wrote in 1943, "About Angelica clings an air of antiquity, a scent of musk and mignonette." The aroma grows fainter, but most noses can still sniff it. Henry W. Clune, the Rochester novelist and upstate New York's grand old man of letters, told me that as a young man he longed to live in Angelica, with its wide maple-lined Main Street and languid pace.

The trees have not moved since Henry's time, nor has the pace quickened. The opening of State 17, the Southern Tier Expressway, has brought more outsiders into Angelica, but it remains somewhat self-contained, said Mayor David Haggstrom as we drank coffee with him in The Little Shop, the Main Street office of the Angelica Booster Citizens.

Though the Mayor's congenial upstate modesty kept him from boasting of it, we later learned that he is one of the finest roque players in Angelica, which means he is one of the best roquers on the planet.

Since the 1860s, roque—a version of croquet featuring tricky rebound shots—has been the game of choice in Angelica. The village park, deeded to Angelica by Philip Church in 1831, sits at the center of town, and within its circular bounds is an octagonal clay roque court—one of only two in the country. For years, old men gathered under the lights at eventide and swung their mallets.

Time passes, traditions fray, and yes, the park today has the usual netless and bent basketball rims above asphalt courts. But roque endures. "We keep it alive for the sake of keeping it alive," says Mayor Haggstrom. Tournaments are held now and then, and if a visitor wants to get up a game he "should just ask around." You need four people to play, and the proper equipment, but a call to the Angelica Booster Citizens beforehand should secure you court time and a quartet.

The park gazebo overlooks the roque court from the west; to the east is the courthouse, which dates from 1819 and hosted New York's first Republican convention back in 1854. The courthouse and surrounding buildings were placed on the National Register of Historic Places in 1978.

Though his town lay considerably east of the county's center, Philip Church was determined to make Angelica the county seat. So he simply annexed three towns from adjacent Steuben County and, voilà, the center had shifted!

Angelica

As later Churches dissipated the family wealth in foolish speculation, and the major railroads bypassed Angelica, the town lost its status as county seat to nearby Belmont. Today the courthouse is given over to local government offices, and the one railroad that did run through Angelica—the Pittsburgh, Shawmut & Northern, or "pretty slow and noisy"—has gone the way of the Pullman porter. Today fewer than 1,000 people live in the village, which looks remarkably unchanged from the early years of our century.

The Angelica Booster Citizens, an energetic civic organization, has put together an excellent brochure to inform your walking tour. Park Circle, which engirdles the village green, contains the impressive Hartshorn home and the yellow church which was converted to a grange hall in 1930.

A mile or so east on Main Street is the Until the Day Dawn Cemetery, where you can find Philip and Anna Church. Also resident is Moses Van Campen, "the Davy Crockett of Allegany County," whose circa-1809 brick home lies just a tomahawk toss beyond Moses himself.

The exploits of Moses Van Campen—frontiersman, Indian fighter, and Philip Church's land surveyor—make James Fenimore Cooper's Natty Bumppo look like Cole Porter. It seems that Moses was constantly being kidnapped by the Senecas and made to run the gauntlet, whereupon he'd ingeniously escape, leaving a slew of dead Indians in his wake. His tombstone reads "A brave officer of the Revolutionary War, An Eminent Citizen and an Enlightened Christian," and whatever his crudenesses, he and his ilk made a civilized life possible for the Anna Churches of their world.

I am speaking of Angelica almost exclusively in terms of the past because visitors will most likely want to drop in on the town during its Heritage Days festival on the first weekend in August. The emphasis is on the bygone days, with guided tours of the historic district and a roque tournament to end all roque tournaments.

Country, Dixieland, and big-band sounds echo from the village green, and the usual savory scents of sausages and popcorn made and vended by civic organizations waft through town. A flea

This charming yellow grange hall was converted from a church during the Depression

market and "Christmas in August," in which local crafters sell yuletide ornaments, enliven Main Street. Call the Booster Citizens in advance to register for the roque tournament; practice up on the old bumper-pool table gathering cobwebs in the basement.

The Allegany County Fair is Angelica's other annual party. Held in mid-July, the fair turned 150 in 1994. The fairgrounds are just off East Main Street before the cemetery.

West Main is the village's commercial hub, with its antique shops ("We're cheap!" one proprietor begged me to tell readers), an art gallery, and restaurants. The American Hotel at the corner of West Main and Olean was built in 1808; by 1879, the *History of Allegany County* called it "dilapidated," but it's still in business.

No one ever called the grand Victorian home of Frank and Clara Smith at 64 West Main dilapidated. A couple from Long Island bought this circa-1886 three-story house in the 1980s and opened the Angelica Inn, a bed and breakfast that also serves light lunches from July to December. I want to call its painted exterior green and purple, but my chromophile wife insists that it's celery and plum.

At any of these establishments you'll want to sample what Angelicans bill as "the best water in New York State." The local aqua won the award in 1988 at the New York State Fair in Syracuse, and to this palate it had a fresh and clean taste.

Across the street from the Angelica Inn is the Angelica Free Library, an attractive Classic Revival dedicated in 1900 by Clara Smith. Stuffed birds and antique firearms—including a rifle owned by Moses Van Campen—are displayed in the vestibule; the Colonial Rooms contain a variety of Angelica artifacts, including Van Campen's surveying instruments.

Hunters and anglers ought to fill their baskets (or car roofs) in Allegany County, with its more than 46,000 acres of state and 2,000 acres of county forestland. A list of stocked lakes and streams is available from the county tourism council. McCarthy's Ranch and Petting Farm on State Road just outside the village puts you on more congenial terms with our quadruped friends.

Outdoorsmen will love Allegany County the year-round, but visitors who prefer loafers and pumps to trout and black bear will

The Angelica Inn built as a residence circa 1886

probably time their visits to coincide with Angelica's Heritage
Days. The echo of a glorious past is a far sweeter sound than the
rumble of trucks bearing radioactive cargo.

Allegany County Tourism Promotion Council, 1-800-836-1869
Angelica Booster Citizens (Heritage Days), 716-466-7930
Angelica Courthouse, 716-466-7928
Angelica Inn, 716-466-3295
McCarthy's Ranch and Petting Farm, 716-567-8110

9

Canton

On US 11, seventy-five miles north of Watertown and twenty-five miles south of Massena.

The autobiographer Frederick Exley hailed from Watertown, the largest city in the north country. He called this land "very northern or Russian—almost steppelike." On a train ride home, described in *A Fan's Notes* (1968), he "began to experience the oddly comforting sensation of ascending to the very top of the world, of rising to some place apart from the fitful concerns and harsh sorrows of men, to a glacial and opaline haven where a man, having been hard-used by the world or having used himself hard, might go and ask himself where things had gone wrong."

You needn't be in the mood for glum introspection to appreciate the charms of northern New York. Yes, the winters are cold and snowy, but they possess a crystalline beauty. And for those creatures whose blood runs warm, there's always July and August.

There is a ruggedness to these parts, so it's somehow fitting, once you get over the incongruity, that Western artist Frederic Remington was born in Canton on October 4, 1861. His boyhood home, which is privately owned, is at 55 Court Street. The Frederic Remington Museum, fifteen miles west at 303 Washington

Street in Ogdensburg, contains a collection of his paintings, sculptures, sketches, and personal effects.

The Remington Museum's riches were a gift of the artist's wife Eva upon her death in 1918, but, according to Frederic's biographers, her "bequest to Ogdensburg did not foster her husband's fame. The museum was inaccessible. No one who wanted to see the art, artifacts, and papers could easily get to Ogdensburg to see them, and no one who was in Ogdensburg wanted to see them." However, you can: the museum is open seven days a week, even in those gelid winters.

Remington, Exley—if you should happen to conceive or give birth to a boy up here, we've got a name picked out for him. (As long as we're mentioning robust American male artists, Thomas Hart Benton, the robustest of them all, painted two murals depicting the settlement of the region; they may be seen at the St. Lawrence-Franklin D. Roosevelt Power Project in Massena, thirty miles north of Canton along the St. Lawrence River.)

Remington did some pen-and-ink drawings for the canoe catalogue issued by his Canton friend J. Henry Rushton, a name revered by sportsmen to this day. Rushton owned a boat shop at the corner of Water and State streets in which he and his employees manufactured cedar lapstrake canoes. In time, he earned the sobriquet of "the Stradivarius of the all-wood canoe."

Since 1961 Rushton enthusiasts have sponsored an annual Canton Canoe Weekend on the first weekend in May. Two races of seven and twelve miles in length are held on the Grasse River, which flows through downtown Canton. In recent years a triathlon has been added, and the weekend is now packed with speeches, awards, exhibits, and a dinner. The gleam in the eyes of these Rushtonites is the eventual creation of a Rushton Canoe Museum in Canton; given their zest and energy, the realization of this dream is only a matter of time.

The town of Canton is more upstate New York than Siberian. A handsome village green is surrounded by a historic preservation district: take special note of the county courthouse on Court

Street, which is constructed of materials native to St. Lawrence County—Gouverneur marble and Potsdam sandstone.

Frederick Exley was not the first distinguished writer to issue from this clime. In the early years of our century the journalist Irving Bacheller, bred in nearby Pierrepont and a member of the St. Lawrence University class of 1882, published more than thirty novels of romance and local color, most famously *Eben Holden*. What was once said of William Cullen Bryant—"He was not a great poet but he was a great American"—applies to Bacheller. North country patriotism animated him all his long life (he lived more than ninety years); one of his lesser novels, *The Light in the Clearing* (1917), eulogized Silas Wright, the closest thing New York produced to an Andrew Jackson.

Wright, a New Englander by nativity and a north country man by choice, was the first lawyer in Canton. He was honest and smart and respected by his neighbors back in that halcyon age when citizens actually knew the men for whom they cast votes. When Wright was elected to the state senate in 1823 the vote in Canton was 199 to one in his favor; so widespread was his reputation as a gentleman that it was rumored that Silas himself cast the only dissenting vote.

He thereafter served in a variety of posts—U.S. Representative, state comptroller, U.S. Senator, Governor—with distinction. In many ways Wright was the opposite number of the ubiquitous William Seward; Wright derided the Erie Canal and other Whiggish internal improvements as lavish business subsidies. He was abstemious when it came to tax dollars—if not to intoxicating spirits.

Silas Wright returned to Canton after being defeated for reelection to the governorship in 1846 by John Young, the Whig from Geneseo. He was widely expected to receive the Democratic presidential nomination in 1848, and had he done so, and won— he surely would've been a stronger candidate than the party's defeated standard-bearer, doughface Lewis Cass of Michigan— the War Between the States may have been averted. Alas, death intervened, and as is so often the case upstate New Yorkers were left holding a bag of wishes and what-ifs.

Silas Wright was a hard-drinking farmer whose Jacksonian faith in the common man burned bright as a north-country summer sun. Poets found him irresistible. Walt Whitman honored him as "a true democratic friend of the people . . . a perfectly upright, honest politician. He never betrayed either his friends or his own conscience."

Legend had it that he was stricken at his plow, a Cincinnatus for the American republic. He actually keeled over in the village post office while getting his mail, but this is as apt a symbol: the great man corresponding with his admirers till the end, drawing sustenance and spirit from them.

John Greenleaf Whittier memorialized Wright:

Man of the millions thou art lost too soon!
Portents at which the bravest stand aghast
The birth throes of a future strange and vast
Alarm the land. Yet thou so wise and strong
Suddenly summoned to the burial bed,
Capped in its slumbers deep and ever long,
Hear'st not the tumult surging over head.
Who now shall rally Freedom's scattering host?
Who wear the mantle of the leader lost?

The St. Lawrence County Historical Association administers the Silas Wright Museum, housed in the lost leader's Greek Revival home on East Main Street. Wright and his wife, Clarissa, purchased this cottage in 1833 and proceeded to enlarge it—in a more felicitous manner than Wright's ally Martin Van Buren was to expand Lindenwald, or so most post-and-beam experts believe. (See Chapter 2.)

The home of the man of the millions passed out of the family in 1890. It was a Universalist church for a while, then a tearoom, and finally a pizza parlor (now *that's* democratic) before the historical association purchased it in 1974. You can no longer order a large cheese, pepperoni, and mushroom, but you can visit the residence of one of our young country's finest statesman on Tuesday through Friday every week of the year except the fifty-second. Some of the furniture and adornments belonged to the Wrights (an Empire mahogany sideboard, Silas's mahogany and birch desk, a portrait of Clarissa); others are period pieces. The second floor is devoted to county history.

The Canton Municipal Building at the corner of Main and Miner streets also contains a small museum of local life; it's open Thursday afternoons between 2:00 P.M. and 4:00 P.M. or by appointment.

The St. Lawrence County Dairy Princess is crowned in the village green on the first weekend in June. A parade, agricultural exhibits, music, and sundry festivities fill the square. A farmers' market occupies the green Tuesdays and Thursdays in the summer.

Where better to celebrate Christmas than in the frozen north? Canton's annual Holiday of Lights brightens the first Friday in December. Trees along Main Street are bestrewn with white bulbs; carolers march to the village green, trilling their seasonal tunes.

This is the hardy and neighborly spirit that Irving Bacheller celebrated. Bacheller's alma mater, St. Lawrence University, chartered by the state of New York in 1856, occupies the southeastern part of Canton. It's a fine liberal arts school that lends itself to leisurely strolls.

The university has put together a helpful walking-tour guide. Among St. Lawrence's outstanding buildings is the Gunnison Memorial Chapel, a 1926 English Gothic designed by architect Bertram Grosvenor Goodhue. If you're around at 5:00 P.M. any weekday you'll hear the Bacheller Memorial Chimes ring their sacral song.

Richardson Hall dates from 1857; Herring-Cole Hall, home to exhibits tracing the university's history, is made of St. Lawrence County sandstone.

Hockey is the sport of choice in these boreal parts; St. Lawrence annually fields (or rinks) a fine Division I team that skates at Appleton Arena; Canton College of Technology, a two-year state school, is a junior college powerhouse.

The far newer Owen D. Young Library is named for the General Electric magnate, RCA founder, and occasional statesman who was for years the university's favorite Titan-son. His daughter, Josephine Case Young, wrote the book-length verse poem "At Midnight on the Thirty-first of March," a fantasy about a north-country town mysteriously cut off from the rest of the world.

John Rezelman, the agricultural writer from Bath, New York, says of the north country: "It is unlike anything else in New York. You can travel great distances and nothing changes. The land, the topography, the feel: it's all the same for miles."

The distances and sense of apartness in northern New York may be small compared to, say, Montana—Frederic Remington knew best—but then Canton really isn't so isolated. It has a pride and awareness that so many of our small towns lack. If even so dolorous a soul as Frederick Exley could lose his harsh sorrows up north, think what rapture a more equable person might find.

Canton Chamber of Commerce (Dairy Princess Festival), 315-386-8255
Canton College (hockey information), 315-386-7335
Canton Town and Village Museum, 315-386-3735
Frederic Remington Museum, 315-393-2425
Rushton Canoe Races, 315-379-9241
St. Lawrence County Chamber of Commerce, 315-386-4000
St. Lawrence-Franklin D. Roosevelt Power Project, 315-764-0226
St. Lawrence University (hockey information), 315-379-5875
Silas Wright House, 315-386-8133

10

Seneca Falls

Take the New York State Thruway to Exit 41 and go south on State 414 for five miles. Or take US 20 ten miles east of Geneva or fifteen miles west of Auburn.

My wife and I call this stretch of State 5 and US 20 "brick alley" because so many homes in Seneca Falls and the neighboring village of Waterloo are of that construction. If you're coming into town from the west, stop and read the historical markers on Waterloo's Main Street. The village claims to be the birthplace of Memorial Day, though this is hotly disputed by Boalsburg, Pennsylvania. It's an old-fashioned New York–Pennsylvania donnybrook, a serious contention but with a leavening levity.

Waterloo eschews the modern convenience of observing Memorial Day on the last Monday of May and instead holds a giant parade, solemn and respectful and bannered with flags, on the real Memorial Day, May 30th. There are no balloons or venders selling confections; Waterloo has been honoring its dead since 1866, and the accumulated weight of memory and loss does not permit the usual frivolities.

The Memorial Day Museum at 35 East Main Street has a century and a quarter's worth of mementos. And they'll tell you that Congress, in May 1966, officially declared Waterloo the birthplace of Memorial Day. Take *that*, Boalsburg.

As residents of Elba, New York, my wife and I feel a Napoleonic kinship with Waterloo, though on the whole, we'd rather be in exile.

Waterloo and Seneca Falls, only three miles apart, are connected by the Seneca and Cayuga Canal, a "feeder" to the Erie which also links two of the sinuous Finger Lakes.

The falls that gave the village its name once cascaded fifty feet, until the engineers sacrificed them to the Moloch of Progress, Clinton's great ditch (see Chapter 1). Then in 1915 the Seneca River and the Seneca and Cayuga Canal were merged; the intentional flooding forced more than 100 factories and commercial buildings and sixty homes to be moved or drowned in a massive relocation that old-timers insist was senseless and destructive. It was, one must concede, an impressive example of man's dominion over nature, but Seneca Falls is identified with women—in particular, the struggle of American women for equal rights in the domain of politics.

History is easiest to understand when it is personalized, and in Seneca Falls the women's rights movement has its apotheosis in a stout and indefatigable nineteenth-century housewife named Elizabeth Cady Stanton.

Elizabeth, daughter of a prominent Johnstown family, moved with her husband Henry, a political activist of independent means, and their three boys to Seneca Falls in 1847. Her father, a justice of the New York State Supreme Court, bought the Stantons a house at 32 Washington Street which they dubbed "Grasmere," in honor of the poet William Wordsworth. Motivated by "the general discontent I felt with woman's portion as wife, mother, housekeeper, physician, and spiritual guide," Elizabeth plunged headfirst into the embryonic women's rights movement.

She and her friend Lucretia Mott organized the convention of July 19-20, 1848 at the Wesleyan Chapel to discuss the "social, civil, and religious condition and rights of women." Elizabeth— just thirty-two years of age—was the principal drafter of "A

82

Declaration of Rights and Sentiments," the convention's call to arms, which was a rewrite of the Declaration of Independence along feminist lines. Among its most outrageous demands was the vote for women—seventy-two years before the ratification of the Nineteenth Amendment.

More than 300 women (and men, notably an ex-slave living in Rochester named Frederick Douglass) attended the Seneca Falls Women's Rights Convention of 1848, which is widely regarded as the pivot point of American feminism, or at least its premodern version. Contemporaries derided it as the "Hen Convention," an assemblage of impractical women and epicene men making foolish demands, but the future held many surprises for the complacent.

Elizabeth remained in Seneca Falls until 1861, when political appointment took her husband to New York City. She returned to the town but once, in 1862, for a speech, and apart from a monument placed upon the meeting site in 1908 by the New York Women's Political Union she went unhonored in her own town, like most prophetesses.

The Seneca Falls Women's Rights National Historical Park was a labor of love for dozens of women (and their male helpmates). Largely due to the efforts of Senator Pat Moynihan, it was given congressional imprimatur in 1980. Its noncontiguous buildings and feminist themes make it one of the more unusual jewels of the National Park Service.

Get your bearings at the visitor's center at 136 Fall Street. The exhibits are informative, and you can pick up useful pamphlets on everything from phrenology to Lucretia Mott. Admire the nineteen full-length bronze statues of convention attendees. In summertime, ranger-guided walking tours of the park begin here.

At the corner of Fall and Mynderse streets is the shell of the Wesleyan Chapel wherein the 1848 convention was held. Desanctified years ago, it was a laundromat until its acquisition by the park in 1985. No one really knows what the chapel's interior looked like in 1848, so the park service has demolished everything but two walls and a roof.

The chapel, or what's left of it, is now a "contemplative

space" in which visitors may meditate on anything from the timeless oppression of women to the glories of a dozen chicken wings and a cold Genny.

The adjoining Declaration Park features a 140-foot-long water wall over bluestone inscribed with the Declaration of Sentiments. The minicataract is designed so that the text can be read.

Elizabeth Cady Stanton's modest Greek Revival home is open for inspection at 32 Washington Street, about a one mile walk for the hardy. It is sparsely furnished—the park service is big on authenticity, and because Elizabeth's belongings scattered to the four winds after her death there was no trunkload of heirlooms. (Like so many of the historical personages we memorialize, Elizabeth was reviled in life and revered in death.)

Park Ranger Phil Moses led us through the house, and her obvious love of Mrs. Stanton informed the tour. Our favorite item was the bronzed cast of their handshake that Elizabeth presented to Rochester suffragette Susan B. Anthony. (Miss Anthony's home at 17 Madison Street in Rochester is a fine small shrine.)

Curiously, an even more famous Seneca Falls woman of the era, Mrs. Amelia Jenks Bloomer, the editor who popularized the baggy "bloomers" as a mode of dress for freethinking women, is largely ignored by the park service. Amelia didn't sign the Declaration of Sentiments; she found it too radical, and her interests pointed her toward temperance and dress reform. Historically speaking, she backed the wrong horses.

Back in the middle of town, at 76 Fall Street, I worried that I might suffocate in the politically correct atmosphere of the National Women's Hall of Fame, but my fears were misplaced. The hall, a nonprofit institution housed, ironically, in an old bank, honors about eighty women (more are added every year) for contributions to the arts, sciences, and other fields of endeavor. Once you get past the shrill four-minute video shown upon entrance, you'll learn as you browse.

Each October, in a ceremony open to the public, notable women are inducted into the Hall of Fame. It's not quite like entrance into the pantheon at Cooperstown yet, but then this hall didn't find a home until 1979. No, sophomores, the inductees are not honored with busts. Their likenesses and biographies and personal effects—astronaut Sally Ride's Challenger insignia, Amelia Earhart's slacks—fill a small gallery. Pick up a telephone and you can hear Bessie Smith bawling the blues.

A rotating exhibit in the back room, changed monthly, features talented nonmale artists. The Hall of Fame, like the other museums in Seneca Falls, is open year-round, though unlike the sites in the national park, it requests—well, strongly suggests—an admission charge.

I am still somewhat uneasy about the whole concept of a women's hall of fame: Willa Cather and Emily Dickinson, to name two members, don't belong in a segregated canon, like talented female baseball players who are good but, after all, just girls. My wife enjoyed the hall well enough but found the whole thing slightly condescending. Judge for yourself.

Women's Rights Convention Days in July turn the village into a strange combination of party town and tutorial. A parade trails down Fall Street, and the usual summertime recreations—a ten kilometer race, women's softball tournament, bands, and quartets—are supplemented by a dramatization of the 1848 convention and a series of tours and lectures.

I sense an uneasy coexistence between the working-class Seneca Falls natives and the feminist activists and intellectuals who have made the town a mecca. As a native-born upstater my sympathies are with the townies, but it'd be nice if both sides stood on common ground now and then. Convention Days are an effort to bridge the gap. (Around the same time, and more conventionally than Convention Days, the Seneca County Fair enlivens Waterloo.)

Women's Equality Day in late August is a less festive, more didactic celebration sponsored by the Hall of Fame. (Among the activities is not a wet T-shirt contest.)

Going eastward on Fall Street, take the left tine of a three-pronged fork to Cayuga Street. At 55 Cayuga stands the Mynderse/Partridge/Becker House, the stunning twenty-three room Queen Anne Victorian mansion that houses the Seneca Falls

Seneca Falls Historical Society

Historical Society. Built in 1855 by Edward Mynderse and exten-sively redesigned in 1880 by the Partridge family (no, not that one), the home was sold for a song to the Seneca Falls Historical Society in 1961 by the last of the Becker sisters.

This is the *ne plus ultra* of small-town American Victorian elegance, with elaborately carved woodwork, gorgeous tiles, and a continent full of china, including a set once owned by President Monroe. Three stained-glass windows by the Boston artist James McPherson depict morning, noon, and night; stare at the bat on the evening window and try not to get the creeps.

Behind the mansion is the Beehive gift shop, decorated in the manner of a nineteenth-century country store. Note the clock tower on the grounds; it was built by Seth Thomas, of Connecticut, in 1895.

The Historical Society sponsors an annual tour of homes in early June and an ice cream social on its spacious and gracious lawn in July. Ride on a carousel or in a horse-drawn carriage. There is also a Victorian Sunday held in late November. We saw several schoolchildren helping out around the manse, and it did our hearts good. Who said this younger generation is going to seed?

You'll want to walk Cayuga Street. The Greek Revival at number 27 was owned by Henry Seymour, one of thirty-two male signers of the Declaration of Sentiments. The 1855 Gothic Revival cottage at 42 Cayuga was a stop on the Underground Railroad. The gabled Gothic Revival at 60 Cayuga Street looks as if Nathaniel Hawthorne might be wandering its staircases, deep in melancholy brooding. Constructed between 1864 and 1866, it's an art gallery; the statue on the front lawn, *Woman in Chains*, is very much at home in Seneca Falls.

According to legend, about half the people who have lived and died in Seneca Falls have been men. Many worked in mills and dug the canal and made pumps that were sold the world over.

You can learn about the vital role waterpower played in the village's growth at the Seneca Falls Urban Cultural Park Visitor Center at 115 Fall Street. The park, one of fourteen UCPs in New York, ignores, for the most part, the reformist history of the village and traces its economic development. For most residents, after all, Elizabeth Cady Stanton is nowhere near as significant as Goulds Pumps, once the nation's chief maker of pumps and fire engines.

The town's three major pump companies eventually coalesced into Goulds Pumps, which is still operating on US 20 as you enter town from the west. It's said that 25 percent of all pumps in use around the world were made in Seneca Falls.

Exhibits also trace the intertwining histories of the Seneca River and the Seneca and Cayuga Canal. You can see that canal as you walk out the back door and picnic in Elizabeth Cady Stanton Park. Sit on the gazebo steps and look across the water at the

Look across the Seneca and Cayuga Canal to the
Seneca Falls Knitting Mill, 1844

Seneca Knitting Mills, which has been clothing folks since this limestone-faced factory was built in 1844.

Those with a developed taste for the Rodney Dangerfield of the piscine world will enjoy the Annual Carp Derby in July. Register at People's Park and stick your pole in the waters of Cayuga Lake or the canal. Anglers with less plebian preferences may submerge their lures at the Seneca County Chamber of Commerce Bass Tournament on Cayuga Lake in June.

What goes better with sauteed carp than a bottle of the grape? The shores of Seneca and Cayuga lakes are verdant with the fruit, which the region's vintners press into wine. Ten miles and more outside town are a gaggle of wineries offering tours and samples. To get a map and wet your whistle with a free gulp of grape juice, stop at the tourist information booth at the intersection of US 20 and State 414. You can't miss it; it's underneath the windmill.

Seneca Falls is actually a bit closer to Cayuga than to the lake whose name it shares, but both are central to the life of the community. You can cruise down the canal and out into the lake on the *Seneca Chief* between June and September. Indeed, you can float leisurely around most of the Finger Lakes on commercial cruises offered by several entrepreneurs.

A mile or so northeast of town on State 89 is the 6,400 acre Montezuma National Wildlife Refuge, which is kind of a layover in the transnational flight of waterfowl going to and fro Canada and the Gulf of Mexico. Bird-watchers are advised to migrate to the refuge; in April, it hosts some 70,000 geese in the avian version of a Fort Lauderdale spring break. A variety of flora and fauna call the swampy haven home; a visitor's center, nature trail, two observation towers, and a 3.5-mile automobile path serve biped visitors.

Hundreds of canallers died of malaria contracted from the Montezuma swamps. Think of them as you swat mosquitoes while squinting for an elusive evening grosbeak.

Finally, before you leave the region, take a quick jaunt over to Auburn, fifteen miles east on State 5, US-20. The William Seward House at 33 South Street is one of our favorite museums in the state. Home to President Lincoln's secretary of state, the man who helped found the Republican party and bought Alaska (once known as "Seward's folly"), the circa-1816 mansion is packed with political artifacts and the odd treasures bestowed on globe-trotting diplomats. New York really was the center of American politics in the nineteenth century, with its fabulously diverse cast of characters and movements, and William Seward was one of its brightest lights. (Some of his belongings have made their way into the Seneca Falls Historical Society's museum.) The Seward House is open Tuesdays through Saturdays in all but the winter months.

"The history of mankind," according to the Declaration of Sentiments, "is a history of repeated injuries and usurpations on the part of man toward woman, having in direct object the establishment of an absolute tyranny over her." True or not, this sentiment gives Seneca Falls a character all her own.

Annual Carp Derby, 315-568-5112
Montezuma National Wildlife Refuge, 315-568-5987
National Women's Hall of Fame, 315-568-8060
Seneca Chief Cruises, 607-546-BOAT
Seneca County Chamber of Commerce, 315-568-2906 or
        1-800-SEC-1848 (also for Waterloo)
Seneca Falls Historical Society, 315-568-8412
Seneca Falls Urban Cultural Park, 315-568-2703
Seneca Falls Women's Rights National Historic Park, 315-568-2991
        (also for Elizabeth Cady Stanton House)
Seward House, 315-252-1283
Women's Equality Day, 315-568-2703

11

Geneseo

$\mathbf{O}$ff I-390, about thirty miles south of Rochester, or on State 63, alone in all its glory.

The Genesee Valley is hill and dale country, with splendid prospects of cornfields framed by evergreens. There are plenty of pungent smells, about which the children can make the usual jokes, and on your way into Geneseo via State 63 south you'll pass the Abbey of the Genesee in neighboring Piffard, where the monks bake and sell bread. You're welcome to stop and sample the ascetic aesthetic.

Geneseo, however, is anything but monkish. It appears, at first glance, to be a charming little college town, much more elegant and less scruffy than most. (The entire village as recently placed on the National Register of Historic Places.)

The Wadsworths have been country squires (at times more like feudal lords) since 1790, when James and William, two enterprising scions of this Connecticut family, crossed the wilderness to claim 2,000 acres of an uncle's land. The Senecas later dubbed James "killer of trees."

Within a few years the brothers owned almost 35,000 acres, the bulk of which was farmed by tenants. Unlike the surrounding counties, which were the province of hardy independent farmers and families, Geneseo and its environs were an enormous land monopoly, more Old World than New.

Opening the valley to mass settlement was the Treaty of the Big Tree in 1797, by which Thomas Morris (son of the famed land speculator, Robert), Jeremiah Wadsworth, and several other officials of the United States Government negotiated with fifty-two Seneca Indians—including Red Jacket, Cornplanter, and Handsome Lake—to purchase virtually all the land west of the Genesee River. The price worked out to be about two and a half cents for each of the nearly four million acres.

Jeremiah was not the last Wadsworth to negotiate a good deal. Several members of the family distinguished themselves in Congress and the diplomatic corps. Perhaps most notable was Senator James W. Wadsworth, Jr., a leading figure in the Republican party between the first and second world wars. Senator Wadsworth was a man of probity and rectitude; he sacrificed his career in the upper chamber by taking a stand against Prohibition in 1926. He and his wife, Alice, the daughter of Lincoln's personal secretary and McKinley's secretary of state, John Hay, were the leading duo opposed to women's suffrage. (Geneseo is most emphatically *not* Seneca Falls.)

The Wadsworths established the Genesee Valley Hunt in 1876, and every fall dozens of hunters "ride to hounds"; horns sound, dogs bark, and the horses and their riders pursue their vulpine quarry. Not many foxes are caught anymore—those captured "are probably sick or tired of life," local historian Irene A. Beale notes—but that's not the point.

The Federal style home that James had built for his bride around 1800, the Homestead, still stands at the southern end of Main Street. Hartford House, at the north end just behind the courthouse, was built in 1835 by James' son, General James Samuel, an unsuccessful candidate for governor in 1862 who was killed at the Battle of the Wilderness two years later. (The General's son, James W. Samuel, Sr., was a colorful autocrat who once fired a farmhand for daring to drive around Geneseo in a Model-T

Ford. When his niece reproved him, James, Sr., accused her of being "a goddam Bolshevik!")

The Wadsworths have always complained of being land-poor, but they've not yet opened the Homestead or Hartford House to tourists. These homes, reputedly grand, can be glimpsed, albeit unsatisfactorily, from the street.

"My country is bounded by the line of the sunrise and the sunset," Major William Allen Wadsworth sniffed a century ago. But even a vain lord has a limited dominion. The deceased Wadsworths sleep in the pioneer Temple Hill Cemetery out Alternate US 20; the secondary school the family endowed in 1827, Temple Hill Academy, is now a private residence across the street from the cemetery.

The academy's descendant, in an admittedly attenuated lineage, is the State University College at Geneseo, an excellent liberal arts college that regularly shows up on lists of the best buys for your collegiate dollar.

The campus is pleasant, though many of the buildings are examples of circa-1965 institutional architecture. A permanent exhibit on the history of the college and its surroundings is based in the Newton Lecture Hall.

The village park at the south end of Main Street, the center of the original settlement in 1790, was a gift of the . . . oh, you know what family.

A block north, at what passes for the village's busy intersection, the Wadsworth Memorial Fountain occupies center stage. The red granite base weighs fifteen tons, and getting it shipped from a Maine quarry to a New York City architect was no mean feat. Atop the fountain is a bear hugging a lamp designed by the French sculptor Antoine-Louis Barye. Two local legends exist, neither verifiable: the ursine memorial was an affectionate tribute to Emmeline ("Auntie Bear") Wadsworth; and the bear will turn to look when a virgin from the college walks by, should that ever happen.

Other surnames do pop up in Geneseo's past. John Young, a

village lawyer, defeated Canton's Silas Wright in the gubernatorial election of 1846. A fine portrait of Young hangs in the Livingston County Historical Museum at 30 Center Street. Like most area politicians, he began his career as an Anti-Mason, then became a Whig, and—if Young hadn't died young—would have been present from the creation of the Republican party.

Housed in an 1838 cobblestone schoolhouse, showcases a varied collection including children's toys of the last century (our favorite: "Speculation," a proto-Monopoly), documents signed by such personages as John Adams and Woodrow Wilson, fire-fighting equipment of pre-shiny-red-engine days and paintings of local eminencies, and the Big Tree itself. In one corner of the middle room sits the chair that James Wadsworth, Jr., used when he served as Speaker of the New York Assembly; on the opposite wall hangs a painting of Red Jacket, regretting that he didn't retain a competent real-estate broker.

The museum grounds contain a section of the original Big Tree, the white oak with a twenty-eight-foot circumference that was felled, not by man's despoiling hand but by the floodwaters of the Genesee River in 1857.

The museum is open Sundays the whole year through and Thursday afternoons in the summer. An ice-cream social is held on the commodious lawn in midsummer. Let the vanilla drip down your chin as you walk in any direction and survey the well-kept homes dating back to the early nineteenth century. Many have plaques inscribed with the year of construction. Geneseo has a strong preservationist element, and deservedly so.

The Livingston County Courthouse, an impressive Classic Revival structure at the northern terminus of Main Street, is worth a walk-through. Arthur Train's fictional lawyer Mr. Tutt, kind of a homespun Perry Mason, worked in "Pottsville," with its "beautiful old courthouse," and the setting was really Geneseo.

The Big Tree Inn at 46 Main Street dates from 1833 and was once owned by the Wadsworths. The lunch business is brisk, the setting is relaxed. And while I'm not recommending lodging places in this book, I can't neglect the Oak Valley Inn at 4235 Lakeville

Road, part of which used to be the county's poorhouse—though the rates have gone up considerably since paupers roamed the grounds. A variety of bars featuring hot chicken wings and cold beer keep the young scholars nourished. These establishments dot Main Street. The thoroughfare is even livelier than usual in July, when the Rotary club sponsors the Geneseo Summer Festival.

Students are especially fond of Fall Brook, a strikingly beautiful small waterfall located just a pebble's skip from the estate of the late Margaret Chanler, who in her youth was one of Henry Adams's doting "nieces" and in her old age was the best-selling author of *Autumn in the Valley*, a memoir of her globe-trotting adventures and restful Geneseo interludes. Fall Brook is out State 63 just south of the campus. You have to be eagle-eyed to see the dirt path leading thereto, and purblind not to see the young lovers enjoying cataract trysts.

Aviation buffs must visit the National Warplane Museum, located just off State 63 at the foot of the campus. You can get right into the cockpit of a World War II or Korean conflict–era bomber or transport. Planes include the famed Boeing B-17 Flying Fortress, C-47 "Gooney Bird," Curtiss C-46, and an alphabet soup of other wartime aircraft.

A Fly-In Breakfast is held every June. The dawn sky literally buzzes with planes, their pilots coming in for hearty fare and shop talk. The earthbound are invited, too, even if your winged chariot is a rusted Chevy Celebrity. A show featuring over 100 World War II aircraft and drawing a crowd in the tens of thousands is held each August; some attenders pitch tents, others bunk in motor homes, and the airborne descend in vintage planes. The museum also hosts occasional flying shows and aviation conclaves.

Admission to the museum is $5 for adults, $1 for kids under twelve, and you're strongly advised to call in advance just to make sure the museum's collection won't be flying the friendly skies of another air show the day you hit town. By the way, the driving force behind the museum has a last name that begins with W.

The Genesee narrows to a slender rivulet around Geneseo. But take State 39 west out of the village and the signs will lead to

More than one hundred World War II aircraft flock to the
National Warplane Museum every August

the river in all its magnificence as it cuts through Letchworth State
Park, which local boosters call "the Grand Canyon of the East." To
these eyes, the Arizona ditch ought to be termed "the Letchworth
of the West." (Henry W. Clune's classic *The Genesee*, recently

96

reissued in paperback by Syracuse University Press, is a perfectly realized history of the river and the people who made lives upon its shores.)

You'll pay three dollars per carload as you drive through one of the park's five entrances. At the Geneseo–Mt. Morris entrance, you'll see the Mt. Morris Dam on your left. Built between 1948 and 1951 to keep the Genesee from its periodic and destructive flooding, the concrete dam is 215 feet above streambed and 1,028 feet across.

And while we're praising famous public works, appreciate the park's many CCC stone benches and cabins and bridges; four Civilian Conservation Corps camps operated within Letchworth during the New Deal, and old-timers still take pride in the structures they built.

The centerpiece of Letchworth is a seventeen-mile-long gorge. Three waterfalls grace the park; the largest is a 107-foot drop, and wouldn't you know, a rich guy bought it.

William Pryor Letchworth, the park's eponym, was a son of prominent Quakers; his father was a friend of Auburn's William Seward, President Lincoln's secretary of state. William made a fortune in the hardware and carriage businesses, then retired to a life of good works and Gilded Age philanthropy. He was an inveterate reformer whose catholic interests included better treatment (in his view) of poor children, prisoners, epileptics, and the insane.

In 1859 he moved to this arboreous retreat and began the rescue of 1,000 lumbering-scarred acres along the Genesee. He oversaw their replenishment from his stately home, at which he entertained friends such as Millard Fillmore. He threw parties for orphans and founded a museum of local history and in general played the kindly lord of the manor, in keeping with the area's traditions.

As a crippled old man, he feared that his beloved valley might fall into the hands of the hydroelectric octopus upon his death. So he performed his final act of charity: he deeded his land to New York State, and it is among our state's most breathtakingly beautiful acres.

Country Towns of New York

Mr. Letchworth's home is now the Glen Iris Inn, which features a restaurant, fifteen guest rooms, and a nice collection of oil paintings, including one of that handsome devil Millard Fillmore. Don't be surprised if you wander into a wedding photo; the inn is a favorite of local newlyweds. It overlooks the Middle Falls; the spray from the whirlpool cooled our brows on an infernal July day. The inn is open from April to October.

A small museum sits just beyond the mist. It contains artifacts of American Indians and settlers, as well as a number of Mr. Letchworth's belongings. A huge mastodon skull and tusk are highlights. The museum is open daily between 10:00 A.M. and 5:00 P.M.; there's no admission fee.

Ranking side by side with the Wadsworths in the history of Geneseo is Mary Jemison, the fabled "White Woman of the Genesee," and Letchworth is her memorial, too. Mary was a fifteen-year old girl when her family was attacked—and most of them killed—by Indians in southern Pennsylvania.

She was spirited away and delivered into the hands of the Senecas, who raised her as one of their own. She married a Delaware Indian and moved with him to the Genesee Valley, a 600-mile trek on foot, with a papoose strapped to her back. Her husband died en route, and Mary wed Hiokatoo, the Seneca chief, forty years her senior, with whom she had six children. When the infamous Sullivan's Raid of 1779 destroyed her village as well as dozens of other Indian settlements, Mary's comrades called it quits and moved west—but Mary stayed on in the valley, farming and dealing with preternatural shrewdness until she had amassed a considerable estate. She—unlike her tribesmen—came out of the Treaty of Big Tree flush with lush land.

Mary's later life was filled with troubles and setbacks and murderous offspring, and she died penurious and landless on a reservation near Buffalo, but her stature grew, even in death, and her name is still spoken reverently. (Our finest historical novelist, Walter D. Edmonds, loosely based his novella *In the Hands of the Senecas* on Mary's ordeal.)

98

Geneseo

William P. Letchworth dug up Mary's bones from a reservation cemetery and reinterred them in the village park in 1874. Mary rests between a log cabin (also relocated by WPL) she built for her daughter Nancy in the early years of the nineteenth century and a pre-Revolutionary War Seneca Council House. The Senecas called Mr. Letchworth Hai Wa Ye Is Tah, or "Man Who Always Does Right," so we'll forbear from criticizing him for disturbing Mary's remains. If they don't mind, I don't mind.

Letchworth offers organized hikes and lectures on everything from American Indians to wildflowers; or be like the late great Ed Abbey and go off on your own down an unbeaten path. You've got over 14,000 acres to play with. Cabins and tent and trailer sites can be reserved.

For those not inclined to Thoreauvian reveries over the berries and the bullfrogs there are plenty of other activities, some free and some pricey: balloon and airplane rides, rafting, and a summer concert series. The park is especially beautiful, as indeed all of upstate New York is, in the early fall.

Upstate writers are of two minds about Geneseo. Carl Carmer loathed its "artificial British class-pattern." The curmudgeonly Carmer sniffed in 1936 that "the relationship between the landed gentry and the countryside is cordial and amusing—but a little as if it were a creation of Gilbert and Sullivan. Perhaps it could better be compared to an English high comedy in which neither the leading players nor the character actors are very sure of their lines or the stage business. It could never be reconciled to any conception of American democracy."

Arch Merrill, on the other hand, insisted that "Geneseo people don't regard themselves as serfs or yeomen in a comic opera English countryside. They like their landed gentry and are proud of them—without any pulling of their forelocks to the squires."

We'll let Henry W. Clune have the last word on Geneseo: "Here the sometimes dubious thing called 'progress' has been restrained; here a blessed peace and pastoral quiet prevail." May they ever in this peaceful valley.

Big Tree Inn, 716-243-2330
Glen Iris Inn, 716-493-2622
Letchworth State Park, 716-493-2611
Livingston County Historical Museum, 716-243-2311
Livingston County Tourism Office, 716-346-6690
National Warplane Museum, 716-243-0690
Oak Valley Inn, 716-243-5570.
SUNY College at Geneseo, 716-245-5873
William Pryor Letchworth Museum, 716-493-2760

12

Westfield

$\mathbf{O}$ff Exit 60 of the New York State Thruway, ten miles north of the Pennsylvania state line.

Welcome to the southwestern jut of New York, where the breeze blows in off Lake Erie and rustles the grapevines whose fruits are alchemized into wine and juice. There are hellacious winter storms and gorgeous summer days and fresh vivifying air.

I visited the pretty village of Westfield with my friend Chuck Ruffino of Fredonia, who first led me on a harrowing cook's tour of the long-abandoned Koch's Brewery in nearby Dunkirk, complete with shattered glass lining blind alleys, scurrying rats under massive vats, and a rickety four-story staircase with strategically placed foot-sized holes. Admission is free, and probably illegal.

Dunkirk, it seems, bet on the wrong libation. Beer led it to ruin, as the temperance ladies always said it would, while its southern neighbor Westfield prospered with its grapy concoctions.

In 1873 a New Jersey dentist and ardent prohibitionist named Dr. Thomas Branwell Welch and his son Charles devised a method of transubstantiating Concord grapes into unfermented wine, suitable for the religious ceremonies of those denominations unfriendly to the more potent variety of the grape. Young Charles worked doggedly and the business grew, until in 1896 he founded a factory on North Portage Street in Westfield. The grape growers of the Chautauqua region, who had theretofore supplied the area's many vintners, now sold much of their crop to the abstemious men of Welch's—which is exactly as the Welches had planned. They were making a handsome profit and keeping thousands of tons of grapes out of the presses and barrels of winemakers.

Charles, whose devotion to the dry cause was such that he ran for governor of New York in 1916 on the Prohibition party ticket, died in 1926, at the height of the nation's experiment in Big Brotherism by the glass. (Some years later, the company that bore his name ventured into the winemaking business in a small way, which must've moved two angry shades to midnight wailings.)

The original brick Welch's plant is on State 394 (North Portage Street), just half a mile from the village's center; my intrepid pal Chuck tried the door of this abandoned plant and—thankfully—found it locked. Across the street is the newer factory, big and green and nondescript.

Poor Charles Welch: his *idée fixe* was a magnificent success, blossoming into a veritable grape-juice empire, yet, judged by his ulterior motive—taking Chautauqua's grapes out of wine production—he was a dismal failure. The county is the wine capital of New York, supplying enough Labruscas and Chardonnay to float a convention of oenophile yuppies.

For those who prefer their grapes fermented, the Vetter Vineyards, out East Main Road, north of Westfield, and the Johnson Estate Winery on US 20 south of town offer summer tours and year-round samples of their product. The Johnson Estate, established in 1961, is a family affair and the oldest exclusively estate winery in the state. The Vetter Vineyards have a gift shop that sells wine-related jellies.

Every town has its myths, tall tales embroidered out of the most homespun cloth, and only a spoilsport would go around debunking them. How refreshing, then, that Westfield's preeminent myth happens to be true—it put the whiskers on Abraham Lincoln's angular face.

Westfield

An eleven-year old girl from Westfield, Grace Bedell, after examining her Republican father's campaign placard, wrote to candidate Abraham Lincoln on October 15, 1860, that he "would look a lot better" if he "wore whiskers." Four days later Lincoln responded, by longhand, that "as to the whiskers, do you not think people would call it a piece of silly affectation if I were to begin it now?"

Four months later, on February 15, 1861, on his journey eastward to take the oath of office, Lincoln's train stopped at the Westfield station. A crowd gathered, and the newly bewhiskered president-elect announced, "I have a correspondent in this place, and if she is present I would like to see her. Her name is Grace Bedell."

Grace made her way through the throng and was lifted up to the platform, where Abe kissed her. "You see, Grace, I let my whiskers grow for you," he said, thus punctuating one of those stories that common sense (and acquired cynicism) tell you must be apocryphal, but aren't. Lincoln later explained that he answered the impudent lass' letter because it "was so unique, and so different from the many self-seeking and threatening ones I was receiving daily, that it came to me as a relief and a pleasure."

Grace occupies an entire exhibition case in the McClurg Museum in Westfield's Village Park. The museum, home to the Chautauqua County Historical Society, is the former residence of a Scots-Irish merchant named James McClurg, whose neighbors mocked this manor as "McClurg's folly" for its grandiosity. Construction began in 1818 on this, the first brick house in a settlement of log homes. In 1935 McClurg descendants left it to the village of Westfield, which turned it over to the society for use as a museum in 1950.

Sixteen rooms are devoted to Chautauqua in the Civil War, the region's American Indians, early kitchenware, and the furnishing and accouterments of a prosperous burgher in the small-town America of the Gilded Age. There is a photograph of an older Grace Bedell, lips curled into the satisfied half-smile of an aging child star

*Once dubbed "McClurg's folly," this charming building
is now a museum*

recalling past glories. "Old Abe Kissed By Pretty Girl," headlined
the *New York Tribune*, and the pretty girl lived in the (still standing)
house at 36 Washington Street, two blocks north of Main.

The interconnectedness of upstate New York is a constant
source of wonder, and William Seward makes a cameo in Westfield,
as he does in so many of these towns. Seward lived in the McClurg
home in the mid-1830s as an agent for the Holland Land Office. His
black-iron safe is on display, as is the wooden shingle his brother
B.J. hung. (How fitting that Auburn's gift to diplomacy, Secretary
of State Seward, whose purchase of Alaska in 1868 was labelled
"Seward's folly," lived in McClurg's folly.)

The McClurg Museum is open between April and November

every day but Wednesday and Sunday. A modest admission fee is charged. The historical society also holds an annual antique show.

The McClurg looks out over the village park; the handsome gazebo and towering churches that border the green make an attractive tableau. St. Peter's Episcopal church dates from 1830; across the grass is the handsome circa-1878 Presbyterian church.

Westfield's Main Street is a hodgepodge of brick storefronts and old-fashioned diners (coffee is free when you buy a piece of pie at one of them) and a dappling of antique shops and cooperatives. The village has become something of a regional antique capital; Buffalonians, Pennsylvanians, and other strange creatures spend happy Saturdays scavenging for escritoires, washboards, settees, and yellowed copies of Poe's first volume.

The dog days of summer are enlivened by one of the larger arts and crafts shows of the area, held on a Friday and Saturday on the commodious town square. Meanwhile, the handiwork of over fifty local artists and artisans is for sale every summer day—weekends only in winter—at the Portage Hill Gallery, located in a circa-1830s Greek Revival home east of town on State 394.

If, by chance, you're hit by a truck, at least you'll have the consolation of being treated at one of the loveliest hospitals in the state. The Westfield Memorial Hospital at 189 East Main Street was built by a doctor in 1853; notice the iron dogs, blacker than Cerberus, guarding the entrance.

South Portage Street is marvelous for walking. An octagon home is at the intersection of Chase and South Portage streets; two blocks north, at 40 South Portage, is the Patterson Library and Art Gallery, a 1908 Classic Revival structure donated by Miss Hannah Patterson in honor of her distinguished parents.

Hannah's father, George Washington Patterson, succeeded Seward as the local land agent and went on to serve as Speaker of the New York Assembly, lieutenant governor, congressman, and a delegate to the 1856 Republican convention. (Outside the cities, upstate was once as solidly Republican a region as existed in the country. The leading men of the towns were often pioneers in the launching of this new party, and when the GOP ship came in they were rewarded with the usual patronage jobs. The first partisan newspaper in America of its allegiance, *The Westfield Republican*, is still publishing.)

The Pattersons lived in a massive Greek Revival home on North Portage Street, which the ubiquitous William Seward built in 1838. The home was moved, pillars and posts, in 1966 to make room for a new grape-receiving station for Welch's. It's now the William Seward Inn, a bed and breakfast out on Portage Road.

Other outstanding homes to look for include the sprawling hodgepodge mansion at 309 East Main Street built in 1870 by Reuben Wright, who struck gold in California; the circa-1829 home with the unusual arched recessed porches on the north side of US 20, three miles west of town; and the circa-1835 hip-roof house at 93 West Main Street, in which members of the Millerite sect, who believed the world would end on October 22, 1844, awaited that long uneventful day.

Back to the Patterson Library. It is magnificent, with a central rotunda and a dome supported by eight large Corinthian columns. An art gallery on the lower level houses rotating shows. A semicircular back balcony overlooks Chautauqua Creek, whose gorge is marked by steep craggy cliffs up to sixty feet in height. You can hike along the creekside paths, which are splendiferous in the gorgeous Westfield autumn.

Hike long enough and you'll encounter the deep blue waters of Lake Erie, two miles northwest of the village. At the corner of State 5 and State 394, surrounded by shrubs and marked with a No Trespassing sign, is the Barcelona lighthouse, a stone tower dating from 1829. The lighthouse was illuminated by natural gas for its first decade, and for a time the harbor battened on the Canadian trade. Then the Erie Railroad honored Dunkirk with its terminus, and in 1857 the lights went out in Barcelona. (They were relumed in 1962.)

The lighthouse stands on private property, barely twenty feet from the road. It overlooks the Barcelona Harbor, from whose marina boats are launched more for pleasure than profit.

Westfield

In a way, no light that dims in Chautauqua County ever really goes out. Lily Dale, the spiritualist community in which it is believed that no one dies—and for a green-hued portrait of Andy Jackson a medium will prove it to you—lies ten miles to the east. Visionaries and ragged prophets have wandered the byways of Chautauqua for upwards of 150 years. The popular ethereal folkie

Erected in 1829 on the shores of Lake Erie, the Barcelona Lighthouse once ran on natural gas

band "10,000 Maniacs" hails from Jamestown, the largest city in Chautauqua County, and in lead singer Natalie Merchant's otherworldly voice you can hear the sweet lunatic melodies of 10,000 numinous Chautauquans. Fortified by grape juice, no doubt, and opening antique shops in bankers' homes.

Chautauqua County Historical Society/McClurg Museum, 716-326-2977
Chautauqua County Vacationlands Association, 716-753-4304
Johnson Estate Winery, 716-326-2191/1-800-DRINK-NY
Lily Dale Assembly, 716-595-8721
Patterson Library and Art Gallery, 716-326-2154
Portage Hill Gallery, 716-326-4478
Vetter Vineyards, 716-326-3100
Westfield Chamber of Commerce, 716-326-4000
The Wool Works, 716-326-2848

Bibliography

Aaron, Jan. *Wine Routes of America*. New York: Dutton, 1989.

Adams, Samuel Hopkins. *Canal Town*. New York: Random House, 1944.

Alexander, Holmes. *The American Talleyrand*. New York: Harper & Bros., 1935.

Auchincloss, Louis. *The Vanderbilt Era*. New York: Scribner's, 1989.

Bacon, Edwin F. *Otsego County Geographical and Historical*. Oneonta: Oneonta Herald, 1902.

Beale, Irene A. *Genesee Valley Events 1668–1986*. Geneseo: Chestnut Hill Press, 1986.

Genesee Valley People 1743–1962. Geneseo: Chestnut Hill Press, 1983.

Burns, James MacGregor. *Roosevelt: The Lion and the Fox*. New York: Harcourt, Brace & World, 1956.

Carmer, Carl. *Listen for a Lonesome Drum*. New York: David McKay Company, 1936.

Carmer, Carl. *My Kind of Country*. New York: David McKay Company, 1966.

Champlin, Charles. *Back There Where the Past Was*. Syracuse: Syracuse University Press, 1989.

Champney, Freeman. *Art & Glory: The Story of Elbert Hubbard*. New York: Crown, 1968.

Clune, Henry W. *The Genesee.* Syracuse: Syracuse University Press, 1963, 1988.

Conover, Jewel Helen. *Nineteenth-Century Houses in Western New York.* Albany, State University of New York Press, 1966.

Cook, Blanche Wiesen. *Eleanor Roosevelt.* New York: Viking, 1992.

Cornell, Thomas D. "The Hammondsport Glen." *Crooked Lake Review.* July 1993.

Costa, Edith L., and Mary H. Biondi. *Top o' the State.* Ogdensburg, New York: Northern New York Publishing, 1967.

Cross, Whitney R. *The Burned-Over District.* Ithaca: Cornell University Press, 1950.

Dilley, Butler F., editor. *Biographical & Portrait Cyclopedia of Chautauqua County, New York.* Philadelphia: John M. Gresham, 1891.

Downs, John P., editor. *History of Chautauqua County and its People.* 3 volumes. New York: American Historical Society, 1921.

Exley, Frederick. *A Fan's Notes.* New York: Random House, 1968, 1988.

Griffin, Elisabeth. *In Her Own Right: The Life of Elizabeth Cady Stanton.* New York: Oxford University Press, 1984.

Irving, Washington. *The Legend of Sleepy Hollow.* Mahwah, New Jersey: Watermill, 1918, 1980.

Kelley, James L., and Lee S. Monroe. *Roy M. Mason.* San Diego: Frye & Smith, 1974.

Lane, Wheaton J. *Commodore Vanderbilt.* New York: Alfred A. Knopf, 1942.

Le Roy Sesquicentennial Historical Committee. *The Heritage of Le Roy.* 1984.

McMahon, Helen G. *Chautauqua County: A History*. Buffalo: Henry Stewart, 1958.

Writers' Program of the Works Progress Administration. "New York: A Guide to the Empire State." New York: Oxford University Press, 1940, 1962.

Niven, John. *Martin Van Buren: The Romantic Age of American Politics*. New York: Oxford University Press, 1983.

O'Connor, Lois. *A Finger Lakes Odyssey*. Lakemont, New York: North Country Books, 1975.

Rayback, Robert J. *Millard Fillmore*. Buffalo: Buffalo Historical Society, 1959.

Roosevelt, Elliott. *The Hyde Park Murder*. New York: St. Martin's Press, 1985.

Roth, Catherine, editor. *The Architectural Heritage of Genesee County*. Batavia: Landmark Society of Genesee County, 1988.

Samuels, Peggy and Harold. *Frederic Remington*. Garden City, New York: Doubleday, 1982.

Swarthout, Laura L. *A History of Hammondsport to 1962*. Hammondsport: Crooked Lake Historical Society.

Vanderbilt, Arthur T., II. *Fortune's Children*. New York: William Morrow, 1989.

Ward, Geoffrey C. *A First-Class Temperament*. New York: Harper & Row, 1989.

Webster, Harriet. *Favorite Short Trips in New York State*. Dublin, New Hampshire: Yankee Publishing, Inc., 1986.

White, Bruce A. *Elbert Hubbard's The Philistine: A Periodical of Protest (1895-1915)*. Lanham, Maryland: University Press of America, 1989.

Wilson, Edmund. *Upstate*. New York: Farrar, Straus & Giroux, 1971.

Wyld, Lionel D. *Low Bridge!*. Syracuse: Syracuse University Press, 1962.

Young, Andrew W. *History of Chautauqua County, New York*. Buffalo: Matthews & Warren, 1875.

Arch Merrill, a Rochester newspaperman, published a score of books about the small towns of upstate New York in the middle years of the century. They contain a good deal of local color and, thanks to numerous reprints, are widely available throughout the region.

Index

Country Towns of New York

114

Index

Country Towns of New York

116

Index